Fallibility at Work

Øyvind Kvalnes

Fallibility at Work

Rethinking Excellence and Error in Organizations

Øyvind Kvalnes
BI Norwegian Business School
Oslo, Norway

ISBN 978-3-319-63317-6   ISBN 978-3-319-63318-3 (eBook)
DOI 10.1007/978-3-319-63318-3

Library of Congress Control Number: 2017948701

© The Editor(s) (if applicable) and The Author(s) 2017. This book is an open access publication and is sponsored by BI Norwegian Business School.
Open Access This book is licensed under the terms of the Creative Commons Attribution 4.0 International License (http://creativecommons.org/licenses/by/4.0/), which permits use, sharing, adaptation, distribution and reproduction in any medium or format, as long as you give appropriate credit to the original author(s) and the source, provide a link to the Creative Commons license and indicate if changes were made.
The images or other third party material in this book are included in the book's Creative Commons license, unless indicated otherwise in a credit line to the material. If material is not included in the book's Creative Commons license and your intended use is not permitted by statutory regulation or exceeds the permitted use, you will need to obtain permission directly from the copyright holder.
The use of general descriptive names, registered names, trademarks, service marks, etc. in this publication does not imply, even in the absence of a specific statement, that such names are exempt from the relevant protective laws and regulations and therefore free for general use.
The publisher, the authors and the editors are safe to assume that the advice and information in this book are believed to be true and accurate at the date of publication. Neither the publisher nor the authors or the editors give a warranty, express or implied, with respect to the material contained herein or for any errors or omissions that may have been made. The publisher remains neutral with regard to jurisdictional claims in published maps and institutional affiliations.

Printed on acid-free paper

This Palgrave Macmillan imprint is published by Springer Nature
The registered company is Springer International Publishing AG
The registered company address is: Gewerbestrasse 11, 6330 Cham, Switzerland

Acknowledgements

While working on this book I have benefitted greatly from the support and encouragement of family and friends, and from the reflections and input from colleagues, students, and professionals who have agreed to meet and talk about fallibility at work. Special thanks to Bjørn Atle Bjørnbeth, Inga Bolstad, Kristine Borvik, Arne Carlsen, Anders Dysvik, Herman Egenberg, Tharan Fergus, Jarle Gimmestad, Ingun Grytli, Thomas Hoholm, Mette Kaaby, Espen Kvark Kvernbergh, Salvör Nordal, Helén Norlin, Erik Osmundsen, Mina Randjelovic, Ingvild Müller Seljeseth, Miha Skerlavaj, Morten Theiste, Ragnhild Elin Thoner, Ósk Vilhjálmsdóttir, Stian Westad, and Torbjørn Aanonsen. I would also like to thank my employer BI Norwegian Business School for funding my work and making it possible to publish it with Open Access.

Contents

1 **Risky Play** 1
  1 Benefits of Risky Play 3
  2 Stoical Approaches 10
  References 17

2 **Failing Fast** 21
  1 Innovation and Failure 23
  2 Beyond Blame 26
  3 Three Obstacles 28
  References 35

3 **Moral Risk in a Nursing Home** 39
  1 Active and Passive Mistakes 41
  2 The Fish Dilemma 45
  3 Moral Hazard and Moral Paralysis 49
  4 Supportive Leadership 52
  References 56

4	**Coping with Fallibility in Aviation**	59
	1 Inattentional Blindness	61
	2 A Barrier Model	63
	3 Beyond Hint and Hope	69
	4 Teamwork	73
	References	77
5	**Fallibility and Trust in Healthcare**	79
	1 Immediate Acknowledgement	81
	2 Barriers in Healthcare	86
	3 Sharing Mistakes	91
	References	97
6	**Approaches to Help in Organizations**	101
	1 Beyond the Crowd	103
	2 Perceived Social Costs of Seeking Help	106
	3 Systems of Holding Back	112
	References	117
7	**Ethics of Fallibility**	121
	1 The Good and the Right	123
	2 Moral Fallibility	129
	3 Moral Neutralization	133
	4 Forgiveness	138
	References	142
Conclusions		147
Index		157

List of Tables

Chapter 1
Table 1   Self-understanding   14
Table 2   Adversity time frame   17

Chapter 6
Table 1   Time frame for help seeking   108

Chapter 7
Table 1   Ethics of fallibility time frame   128

Introduction

Pilot Jarle Gimmestad sat in the cockpit at Oslo Airport one late evening, waiting for takeoff. "The flight was already delayed by one hour, and I was eager to get onto the runway. As usual, I was in dialogue with the co-pilot to make final adjustments before takeoff. Suddenly, the driver of the pushback tractor on the ground drew our attention to a wet substance that dripped from one of the wings and onto the asphalt below. It had already formed a stain on the ground. The driver hinted that there could be an oil leak from the wing or motor. He suggested that we should get the motor engineers out to identify the cause of the dripping." Gimmestad talked with his co-pilot about it. Together they concluded that the stain was too small to give cause for alarm, and continued to prepare for takeoff.

The pushback tractor driver was still concerned about the dripping. Now he started to count the number of drops per minute that still came from the wing, and reported it to the men in the cockpit. He also measured the size of the stain on the asphalt, to indicate how serious he thought the matter was. Gimmestad suggested to him that contributions to the stain on the ground could have come from other planes that had been parked on the same spot earlier in the day. It is normal to find such stains near the gate: "I tried to get the driver down below to accept that explanation, but he was not convinced. Now I suggested that the substance dripping from the wing probably was only water, and nothing to worry about. I asked the driver to sniff the substance. He did that, and his verdict was that it had a chemical smell, and so was not water."

Gimmestad took in this information, talked with the co-pilot again, and decided to continue and get ready for takeoff. He had now taken the matter from an operations level, where you listen to advice and suggestions, to a leadership level, where the person in charge has to take an authoritative decision. With this move, dialogue and reflection close down, to be replaced by monologue and action: "Conditions are acceptable, we proceed to takeoff." The driver of the pushback tractor should now have understood that the matter was out of his hands, and closed. Instead, he persisted to voice his worry about the state of the plane. After a few seconds of hesitancy, he said: "Do you know what? I don't think you should do that." This remark woke up the pilot and got him to reconsider. Signals from the unassuming but persistent man on the ground finally got through to him. The pilot postponed takeoff and asked the motor engineers to do a thorough investigation of the source of the substance dripping down from the wing.

Once Gimmestad had made that decision, he left the cockpit and went down the stairs to talk to the man on the ground. "When we stood face to face, I got the impression that the driver thought I was angry and would reprimand him. Instead, I shook his hand, and thanked him for his professional behavior. I told him that exactly this sort of behavior is crucial in a proper safety culture." The driver of the pushback tractor does not have a formal role in the safety procedures leading up to takeoff. His sole job is to push the plane out of the position at the gate. He is normally not part of the ongoing dialogue, and as such has to impose himself and take a step forward to demand attention, outside the normal procedure. In this particular case, the driver addressed his concerns to the pilot in an apologetic manner, downplaying his own importance, but at the same time repeatedly insisting that his observations should be taken seriously.

Reflecting afterward on his own behavior, Gimmestad noted how he had addressed both the co-pilot and the man on the ground with the intention of getting confirmation of his own interpretation of the situation. "I did not ask them the open question 'what do you think?' but rather sought support for the way I saw the situation. I said: 'it is probably a stain from other planes, don't you think?'." From his standpoint, the incident served as a reminder of how necessary it is to seek out and be open to other people's perspectives on the same situation (Gimmestad, 2016).

Fallibility is the tendency people have to make mistakes and errors, in the shape of small or large slips, mishaps, and blunders. Some of them can lead to serious harm, while others can create breakthroughs in experimental processes. One particular mistake can thus be the source of harm and frustration, while another can give cause to rejoice, even for the person who made it. The purpose of this book is to explore how the handling of fallibility affects the quality of what people try to achieve together at work. My motivation for doing research in this field is a curiosity about how human beings cope with fallibility at work, both on individual, group, and organizational levels.

The book builds on interviews with professionals from a variety of fields, including healthcare, aviation, public governance, engineering, waste management, and education. I have conducted (1) initial interviews and conversations with them, (2) written down their statements and made preliminary interpretations based on theory, and then (3) sent the texts to the informant to get his or her feedback, (4) written new versions based on that input, and (5) got the informant to read and comment on that version, before (6) finalizing the text from the meetings with that particular informant. With some of the informants, the process of reaching out for narratives and interpreting them has gone on for several years, with others the process has taken three to four months.

I interpret the narratives about fallibility at work in the light of theoretical input from philosophy, psychology, and pedagogy, as these contribute to the understanding of organizational behavior. The discussion in this book is also relevant for leadership theory and positive organizational scholarship. I find theoretical tools and resources in those approaches, and build and expand on them. The book reaches out to fellow researchers who share my curiosity about fallibility dimensions of organizational behavior, and to practitioners in the fields where I have been doing my research, and more generally in organizations where it is important to cope with fallibility.

The narratives of fallibility that you find in this book vary in scale and scope. I interpret them as attempts to make meaningful connections between past, present, and future events. Narratives about change have previously been interpreted in the same manner (Rhodes, Pullen, & Clegg, 2010). At the core of a narrative about fallibility, we often find one critical event. A person appears to be making a mistake and it can set in motion a causal chain of events that either is stopped through human intervention, or develops into some dramatic outcome, either negative or positive. The term I will use for this kind of event is a *critical quality moment*, since the response or lack of it to the initial act will determine the quality of the work or outcome that emerges. The narrative about that moment can then focus on (i) what happened ahead of it, (ii) the moment itself, or on (iii) what takes place afterward.

In the narrative about the pilot and the driver of the pushback tractor, there is (i) an unmentioned past, which consists in a common history of being trained in Crew Resource Management (Gordon, Mendenhall, & O'Connor, 2012; Stoop & Kahan, 2005), a preparation method applied in aviation, (ii) the critical quality moment or event itself, where the driver decides to persistently challenge the pilot about the dripping, and (iii) a brief encounter after the event, where the pilot acknowledges the initiative from the driver. It is also a part of the aftermath that Gimmestad spread the word about the encounter, to further confirm and strengthen the existing communication climate of intervening across rank about serious incidents.

I have my academic training from philosophy, and the starting point for my reflections on fallibility at work is Socrates' motto "Know yourself". On the evidence of Plato's dialogues, where Socrates was the main protagonist, he dismissed the idea put forward by fellow Athenians that he was the wisest of men, and instead advocated the view that all human knowledge is fallible. None of his interlocutors in the dialogues is able to convince him that they are any better, since their claims to wisdom do not hold up under critical scrutiny. Socrates, at least, admits that his beliefs about the world and society may turn out to be false, and so he may be the wisest, in the sense that he realizes the limitations in his own convictions and beliefs about the world (Plato, 1966).

There is a Socratic quality to the intervention from the pushback tractor driver at the airport, a willingness to challenge a person in power, in the name of doing things right together. He persists with his questioning even after he has experienced rejection and irritation from the higher ranked person on the receiving end of his messages. Socratic philosophy is practical at heart, both in the sense that it can address concrete questions about how one should act and live, here and now, and in the wider sense of being oriented toward the goal of leading a richer and better life. It rests on an assumption that an examination of personal beliefs, desires, and habits can lead to significant breakthroughs of knowledge regarding how to live a good life. You may come to realize that your current priorities and ways of living are not consistent with what you actually value and see as important, and so have reasons to make changes.

We can interpret "Know yourself" as a recommendation to look inwards, to examine one's own feelings, desires, commitments, preferences, and habits. Another interpretation of the Socratic motto is that the process of attaining self-knowledge requires you to look outwards, and take note of your own place and role in a community. Who are you among these people? How is your life and your aspirations connected to what other people are attempting to do in their lives? This relational dimension of being a person can be lost if Socrates' motto is understood solely as an exercise in inward meditation on what matters in one's own life. Self-examination in the Socratic sense can consist in an inward and an outward orientation. The former may be the one that springs to mind when we read the motto in isolation, but the latter discloses the social dependencies of human endeavors, and is essential in attempts to understand fallibility at work.

A Socratic examination of life at work can consist of asking questions that highlight relational and collaborative aspects: How is what you are trying to achieve at work dependent upon your colleagues' efforts? How is what your colleagues are trying to achieve at work dependent upon your efforts? These questions address what Dutton (2003) has called high-quality connections at work. Recent research in organizational behavior documents the significance of helping and supportive behavior at work (Grant, 2014). Organizations differ in how employees perceive the threshold for asking for and offering help, and also in the degree to which employees and leaders alike hold back due to the apparent social cost of such activities (Lee, 2002; Wakefield, Hopkins, & Greenwood, 2014). To ask for help is to admit personal limitations, vulnerability, and dependence on others. The Socratic questions emphasize teamwork and collective effort, and can trigger a lowering of the threshold for reaching out to others, asking for help and offering it.

The book consists of seven chapters. Each of them addresses aspects of fallibility at work through the threefold temporal model of establishing connections between past, present, and future.

Chapter 1 focuses on childhood as preparation for adult life where fallibility is likely to be a significant feature. Research suggests that the extent to which children are allowed to engage in risky play will affect their ability to cope with adversity in adulthood. Protective parents and institutions can give priority to the children's safety, and restrict their scope of action in order to reduce the risk of harm. In doing so, the adults may also inhibit what has been called the anti-phobic effects of risky play, a process of releasing the children from phobias that have a significant purpose in early childhood, but will restrict them later in life (Sandseter & Kennair, 2011). The chapter explores the connections between childhood research and the concepts of (i) resilience, (ii) growth mindset and (iii) alternative self-understandings where people primarily see themselves either as agents or pawns, all of which are relevant in the context of coping with fallibility at work.

Chapter 2 discusses fallibility as a dimension of innovative processes. Leaders and organizations tend to assume that failure is always bad, and thus restrict experimentation that is required to learn and develop (Edmondson, 2011). The main narrative under scrutiny is about the decision to stop a large IT-project, despite the resources already invested in it. The principle of failing fast, of admitting that a particular idea or project is not as good as initially thought, makes theoretical and practical sense, but is difficult to implement. The chapter introduces three obstacles to admitting defeat and stopping a project: (i) the sunk-cost fallacy, (ii) the bystander effect, and (iii) the confirmation fallacy. All of these are well-established concepts in explaining human irrationality, and here I apply them in the context of fallibility at work.

A nursing home is the setting for the narrative in Chap. 3. It explores a positive turnaround in that organization based on a raised level of activities involving the employees and residents. Kristine Borvik and Helén Norlin became leaders at the nursing home, and set out to respond to the old people's wish to come closer to life and not be isolated in their rooms. In doing so, they shifted emphasis from a proscriptive ethics (avoid harm) to a prescriptive ethics (do good). The chapter brings attention to the distinction between active mistakes (doing something you should not have done) and passive mistakes (not doing something you should have done), and how the latter appear to be tolerated more. It also discusses how perceptions of the extent to which one will have to take the burden for bad outcomes of one's own actions affect the readiness to take risks at work.

Chapter 4 investigates developments in aviation regarding fallibility, and builds on interviews with pilot Jarle Gimmestad and studies of relevant research. A barrier model for thinking about fallibility dominates the learning processes in this field (Reason, 1990). It distinguishes between actions and their outcomes, and how there is a need for a barrier system to stop the causal chain of events put in motion by a mistake. The obstacles discussed in Chap. 2 can help to highlight the weaknesses in the human dimension of a barrier system. Witnesses to a mistake may fail to intervene due to (i) sunk-cost bias, (ii) bystander effects, and (iii) confirmation fallacies. In addition, the tendency to tolerate passive mistakes more than active mistakes, described in the nursing home context of the previous chapter, poses a challenge to the reliability of the system.

The two main informants for Chap. 5 are experienced doctors, who convey narratives about coping with and learning from failure. Doctor Stian Westad encountered a situation where a mistake by his team led to the death of a baby. With the permission of the parents, he has shared the details of that tragic event with the author of this book, and in other public settings. Doctor Bjørn Atle Bjørnbeth has established a biweekly complication meeting at the unit he leads, to talk about operations and treatments that have not gone as desired or expected. Both doctors focus on how failures and mistakes offer unique learning opportunities. The barrier system described in Chap. 4 is applicable to dramatic situations in healthcare, where a doctor or nurse may make a mistake, and human intervention can stop the causal chain it sets off toward a bad outcome. Trust is an overarching concept for explaining why it makes sense to work systematically to learn from failure in healthcare, since it is an expression of professionals' ability, benevolence, and integrity in relation to their patients.

A dramatic event in a river in Oslo is the starting point for Chap. 6, which addresses helping behavior as an integral dimension of coping with fallibility at work. A swimmer is stuck in the stream, but is reluctant to ask people on the shore for help. He behaves similarly to professionals who want do demonstrate independence and autonomy by performing their tasks without support from colleagues, even when they are struggling and unsure about the way forward. Research indicates that people tend to perceive requests for help to have a considerable social cost (Lee, 2002). Refusals to ask for and offer help at work can be systemic, and based on assumptions about what other people would be willing to do for you (Hämäläinen & Saarinen, 2007). In order to deal adequately with their own fallibility, professionals need to challenge such systems, and take the first steps needed to establish and normalize acts of helping at work.

The final chapter of the book provides the outline of an ethics of fallibility. It contains a normative and a descriptive dimension. The former addresses the extent to which honesty is the right response in situations where a person has made a mistake. Consequentialism and duty ethics offer conflicting advice to a decision-maker who can choose to own up to the mistake or keep it hidden. The latter dimension provides an explanation of what I will call moral fallibility, instances where a person acts contrary to his or her own moral convictions. Developments in moral psychology provide reasons to explain moral misconduct in terms of circumstances rather than character. We can combine the normative and descriptive dimensions of an ethics of fallibility in a stance on the subject of forgiveness. Considerations of whether a person who has made a moral mistake ought to be forgiven (a normative issue) can be informed by knowledge about why people make such mistakes (a descriptive issue).

The threefold temporal model of thinking of fallibility in terms of past, present, and future appears throughout the book. The opening chapter emphasizes how experiences in childhood can serve as preparation for an adult working life involving critical events connected to one's own or colleagues' fallibility. The closing chapter is the most future oriented, since it discusses the extent to which people who have made mistakes deserve to start with a blank page and a new chance to do good work in the company of colleagues. The chapters in between all dwell on preparation, action, and retrospective learning in connection with critical quality moments, and conceptual input that can strengthen our abilities to cope with fallibility at work.

References

Dutton, J. E. (2003). *Energize your workplace: How to create and sustain high-quality connections at work*. New York, NY: Wiley

Edmondson, A. C. (2011). Strategies for learning from failure. *Harvard Business Review, 89*, 48–55.

Gimmestad, J. (2016, 18th November). *Interviewer: Ø. Kvalnes*.

Gordon, S., Mendenhall, P., & O'Connor, B. B. (2012). *Beyond the checklist: What else health care can learn from aviation teamwork and safety*. Ithaca, NY: Cornell University Press.

Grant, A. M. (2014). *Give and take: Why helping others drives our success*. London: Penguin Books.

Hämäläinen, R. P., & Saarinen, E. (2007). Systems intelligent leadership. In *Systems intelligence in leadership and everyday life* (pp. 3–38). Systems Analysis Laboratory, Helsinki University of Technology.

Lee, F. (2002). The social costs of seeking help. *The Journal of Applied Behavioral Science, 38*(1), 17–35.

Plato. (1966). *Apology* (H. N. Fowler, Trans.). Cambridge, MA: Harvard University Press.

Reason, J. (1990). *Human error*. Cambridge: Cambridge University Press.

Rhodes, C., Pullen, A., & Clegg, S. R. (2010). 'If I should fall from grace…': Stories of change and organizational ethics. *Journal of Business Ethics, 91*(4), 535–551.

Sandseter, E. B. H., & Kennair, L. E. O. (2011). Children's risky play from an evolutionary perspective: The anti-phobic effects of thrilling experiences. *Evolutionary Psychology, 9*(2), 257–284.

Stoop, J. A., & Kahan, J. P. (2005). Flying is the safest way to travel: How aviation was a pioneer in independent accident investigation. *European Journal of Transport and Infrastructure Research, 5*(2), 115–128.

Wakefield, J. R. H., Hopkins, N., & Greenwood, R. M. (2014). Help-seeking helps. *Small Group Research, 45*(1), 89–113.

1
Risky Play

We were going to climb a birch, and my best friend started first up the tree trunk. I waited on the ground, to see which branches he chose to step on, in preparation for my own foray towards the top. Suddenly he lost his grip and fell. When he came to a stop, he let out a high pitch scream. As I drew closer, I could see that the tip of a branch was inside his mouth. He had been pierced right through the cheek by a dry branch sticking out from the trunk. In great pain, he managed to maneuver himself away from the tree, with blood running from the wound in his face.

Most of the narratives in this book are from organizational life and collected through interviews, but this one is personal. During my childhood in a suburb of Norway' capital Oslo in the 1960s and early 70s, it was normal for children to roam our neighborhoods and explore the world from different heights and perspectives. We sought adventure and excitement, and the adults tended to ignore our potentially harmful encounters with trees and branches. I can still vividly remember my friend's scream and the sight of the tip of the branch inside his mouth. That dramatic incident put both him and me in a state of temporary shock, but a few days later, we were making further daring ventures towards the treetops. Researchers have explored whether people who have had dramatic falls in childhood tend to be more afraid of heights than other adults, and have found no indication that they are. Fallers seem to put the falls behind them, and even express less fear of heights than those who lack experience of falling (Poulton, Davies, Langley, Menzies, & Silva, 1998).

The freedom to climb that I experienced as a child was part of a more general freedom to roam and be away from our parents' gaze for long spells. At the age of seven, I could be away from my home for hours, without my parents knowing where I was, with whom, what we were doing there, and when I would return. Today, seven-year olds in the same area do not have nearly the same opportunity to move beyond the home or the gaze of adults. If a mother and father today had been similarly unaware of their child's whereabouts, it would most likely have been seen as something the local child welfare authorities should look into. The restrictive tendency is present in many cultures (Francis & Lorenzo, 2006). Evolutionary childhood studies suggest that it may inhibit children's mental and physical development (Sandseter & Kennair, 2011).

This chapter explores how the upbringing of children can affect the extent to which they are capable of and prepared to deal with risk, uncertainty, and fallibility in adulthood. More specifically, it discusses how children's engagement in risky play can prepare them for encounters with real and probable adversity as adults, and also the critical quality moments where the next decision they make will crucially impact the outcome of processes at work. The aim of the chapter is to consider possible links from findings in childhood research to theories about people's capabilities to cope with fallibility in work settings. First, it discusses research on beneficial effects of children's engagement in risky play, most notably the anti-phobic effects of such activities (Sandseter & Kennair, 2011). Second, it draws parallels to three sets of concepts that are relevant with regard to how people prepare for, deal with, and rethink their roles in critical events where mistakes and errors occur. All of them have roots in stoical philosophy, in that they highlight the need to meet adversity with a calm and collected attitude. They are (i) resilience understood as the capacity to bounce back from adversity (Goldstein & Brooks, 2005; Luthar, Cicchetti, & Becker, 2000;

Masten, Best, & Garmezy, 1990), (ii) the distinction between a growth mindset and a fixed mindset, where the former sees mishaps as opportunities for further learning (Dweck, 2017), and (iii) the distinction between agent and pawn (Nygård, 2007) as possible ways to understand oneself and one's role in the way situations and events unfold.

1 Benefits of Risky Play

Risk is the possibility that something unpleasant or unwelcome will happen. Risk is a situation involving exposure to danger (*Oxford living dictionaries*, 2017). Despite the negative connotations of the concept, risk is attractive in many settings. Children climb trees and engage in others kinds of risky play to gain immediate excitement and thrill. It can be great fun, and often creates ecstatic feelings of mastery and self-control. Childhood research indicates that children also benefit from such activities in long-term and unintentional ways (Cevher-Kalburan & Ivrendi, 2016; Greve, Thomsen, & Dehio, 2014; Lavrysen et al., 2017; Sandseter & Kennair, 2011). Climbing trees and rocky hills provides the opportunity to develop and enhance different motoric and physical skills, and for developing muscle strength, endurance, and skeletal quality (Bjorklund & Pellegrini, 2000; Byers & Walker, 1995; Pellegrini & Smith, 1998). Play in heights also provides opportunities to develop competencies to perceive depth, form, shape, size, and movement (Rakison, 2005), and general spatial-orientation abilities (Bjorklund & Pellegrini, 2002). These are significant skills and competencies both for survival in childhood (immediate benefits) and for handling important adaptive tasks in adulthood (deferred benefits).

One of the unintended and deferred benefits of exposure to risky scenarios in childhood can be to create a foundation for understanding and coping with risk at work. Familiarity with risk can be a foundation for becoming constructively involved in innovative processes, for taking chances in situations where you cannot know whether things will turn out well or badly. It can also be a necessary precondition for being at ease and functioning well in professions where things might end up badly, as in healthcare and aviation. A professional must face critical circumstances at work with a calm attitude, and exposure to dangerous situations in childhood may serve as essential preparation for that kind of work.

In childhood research, risky play has been defined as:

> thrilling and exciting forms of play that involve a risk of physical injury. Risky play primarily takes place outdoors, often as challenging and adventurous physical activities, children attempting something they have never done before, skirting the borderline of the feeling of being out of control (often because of height or speed) and overcoming fear. Rather than the avoidance inducing emotion of fear, a more thrilling emotion is experienced. Most of the time risky play occurs in children's free play as opposed to play organized by adults. (Sandseter & Kennair, 2011, p. 258)

From this theoretical perspective, risky play is a necessary condition for learning to cope with potential danger and harm. Evolutionary childhood research indicates that children learn to judge risks through experience with risky situations. Through risky play, they can develop the cognitive skills needed to make more accurate judgements about the circumstances they face (Plumert, 1995; Plumert & Schwebel, 1997). A greater amount of direct experience with a risky situation itself can explain why some individuals demonstrate lower, and more realistic, risk appraisals in particular situations (DiLillo, Potts, & Himes, 1998). Exposure to risky situations appears to strengthen the ability to manage the risk (Adams, 2001) and to enhance the development of a more sound and reliable sense of the actual risk in the situation (Ball, 2002; Plumert, 1995).

Research on childhood indicates that children's freedom to engage in risky and adventurous activities in uncontrolled settings has decreased in the past decades (Francis & Lorenzo, 2006). In the USA, children's involvement in outdoor play has decreased dramatically (Clements, 2004). In Norway, a country with a tradition for a relaxed attitude towards risky play, more elaborate restrictions are gradually introduced to promote childhood safety (Sandseter & Sando, 2016). In many societies, the physical and social space for children to play in has shrunk considerably. Attitudes to parenthood and protection have changed, leading to more emphasis on safety and keeping children away from danger. If parents today had given their child the amount of freedom that children had some decades ago, they would most likely come under criticism for negligence and bad, irresponsible parenting. Concerned neighbors may have found a reason to contact child welfare authorities about it. You are not supposed to let your seven-year old out of sight for long periods of time, at least not when there are no other adults present to take over your role as controller and protector.

When Lenore Skenazy in 2008 gave into her nine-year old son's intense wish to travel home alone from the supermarket on the metro in New York, and wrote about it, she caused controversy and was criticized for being an irresponsible parent.

> For weeks my boy had been begging for me to please leave him somewhere, anywhere, and let him try to figure out how to get home on his own. So on that sunny Sunday I gave him a subway map, a MetroCard, a $20 bill, and several quarters, just in case he had to make a call.
>
> No, I did not give him a cell phone. Didn't want to lose it. And no, I didn't trail him, like a mommy private eye. I trusted him to figure out that he should take the Lexington Avenue subway down, and the 34th Street crosstown bus home. If he couldn't do that, I trusted him to ask a stranger. And then I even trusted that stranger not to think, "Gee, I was about to catch my train home, but now I think I'll abduct this adorable child instead."
>
> Long story short: My son got home, ecstatic with independence. (Skenazy, 2008)

The overwhelming response Skenazy received to this initiative—both supportive and critical—motivated her to create a free-range kid project, devoted to giving parents and others ideas about how to create space for children to develop autonomy and self-respect. Similar initiatives have taken place in other countries as well, countering a development where anxious parents and strict authorities limit children's space to roam, in the name of safety and protection.

Childhood researchers are concerned about a tendency among authorities, professionals, and parents to overprotect children. So-called cotton-wool children are kept at arm's length from anything that might hurt them, but these well-meaning measures can severely limit their mental and physical development. Risky play can have an important and positive anti-phobic effect on children, one they cannot reap from other sources (Sandseter & Kennair, 2011). By climbing trees, using sharp knives, and going for walks by themselves, children can gradually free themselves from phobias about heights, sharp objects, and being left behind by one's group. These are phobias that serve a purpose for very small children but it is good for their mental and physical health to gradually discard them as they grow older. Overprotection can take away the possibility to experience individual growth and development:

> The child may not experience that he or she naturally can cope with the fear-inducing situations. And despite having matured mentally and physically enough to master the previously dangerous situations, one may continue to be anxious. Continued anxiety hijacks the adaptive function of fear and causes non-adaptive avoidance of situations that *were* but no longer *are* dangerous for the individual due to maturation and increased skills. (Sandseter & Kennair, 2011, p. 263)

When we restrict the possibility for risky play, we also take away opportunities to approach adulthood free of the primary anxieties about how things might turn out badly. The research suggests that children need freedom to explore the world on their own, without adult supervision and control, even at the cost of increasing the risk of harm.

Risky play can be placed in six categories (Sandseter, 2007a). They are activities connected to great heights, high speed, dangerous tools, dangerous elements, rough-and-tumble, and disappearance/getting lost. Each of them can have relevance for the development of abilities and skills necessary in adulthood and professional settings, and in coping with fallibility at work. A common feature in all six categories is that there is a real and serious chance that the child can get harmed, and that it is a healthy thing to initially fear the source of this danger. It is the gradual movement out of this state of fearing, through risky play, that can prepare the individual for an adult life where some of the most thrilling and fruitful activities involve risk of harm. Human flourishing, the development of capabilities to change and improve aspects of the world, depends on a gradual release from phobias that are designed to serve us well in early childhood, in order to take chances and only have limited possibility to assess whether things will go well or badly.

The evolutionary explanation of risky play is that it helps to release children from phobias. It can be helpful to look at the possible anti-phobic effects within one of the six categories to establish a connection to risky work in adulthood. Children enjoy walking off alone to explore their environment away from the supervision of parents or other adults (Sandseter, 2007b). They experience a feeling of being lost and left behind by their group when they do so, but still have an urge to do it. Separation is both thrilling and scary. It would be safer for them to stay with the adults, but even so, they drift off on their own, and crave for the particular sense of excitement that comes from being on the move alone (Sandseter, 2007a). It seems that the anti-phobic effect of play where children can disappear and get lost is that they can gradually learn not to fear separation. Small children have good reasons to fear being left on their own and getting away from their closest, as they depend on the adults to feed, shelter, and support them. As they grow older, they can become more independent and autonomous, through being able to explore their environment on their own, without the adults' gaze following them around. The fear of being left behind by the group can be reduced through risky play initiated by the children themselves. "When having the opportunity to voluntarily plan and carry out a separating from their caretakers by exploring new and unknown areas, experiencing the thrill of the risk of being lost, children seem to "inoculate" themselves from the anxiety of separation" (Sandseter & Kennair, 2011, p. 270).

Overprotective parents can do their children a disfavor by sabotaging these expeditions into the unknown. With technology at hand, parents have ways of keeping track of where their children or teenagers are at any moment. One example is the app Bsafe that allows parents to locate the whereabouts of their children at any time, as long as they keep their mobile phones on. The slogan for this device is "the end of worry"

("Webpage for Bsafe,"), and the rationale is to give concerned parents a sense of security and control regarding their children. They do not have to worry that their son or daughter will be next headline in the news about abducted or lost children. The app also offers a sense of protection to the children, who know that no matter where they are, their parents have them on the radar, and can come to their rescue, if necessary.

Under such conditions, the children can only gain limited anti-phobic effects from roaming the neighborhood and beyond, since they are aware that the parents can constantly check where they are, and call them back or collect them there at any time. The beneficial inoculation from the anxiety of separation is unlikely to take place. Concerned, loving, and well-meaning parents can thus block their children's path towards maturity, and restrict their opportunities to learn to cope with being away from their group. As is the pattern with other dimensions of risk, the children who are protected in this way may continue to be afraid of the circumstances they find themselves in, even when they have reached an age where they would normally feel comfortable in them.

In work settings, to suffer from separation anxiety can be a considerable handicap. It is difficult to flourish and do well in an organization if you are constantly afraid of being left alone, and nervous about not being seen or appreciated by your leaders or colleagues. Individuals who have been allowed the thrill of exploring the world on their own in childhood, are more likely to be comfortable with situations at work where they are expected to enter the unknown territory and report back later about what they find there.

Some researchers and commentators that support the initiative to give children more freedom and space for play are unhappy with the concept of "risky play". They believe that "risky" has negative connotations, and prefer to talk about the adventurous and challenging play:

> If something is deemed 'risky', the risks are understood to be excessive. *Such activity is best avoided.* Inviting parents to encourage their children to do things that are expressly risky is simply counterintuitive: where children are concerned, the instinct to protect is too profound. (Voce, 2016)

As we attempt to move towards allowing children more freedom to explore their world, the emphasis on the word "risk" shows that we still haven't let go of the mindset of the helicopter parent who is more aware of danger than adventure, more focused on what could go wrong than how to prepare kids to be both independent and safe in challenging situations.

So, please, can we stop talking about risk? Instead, let's talk about adventure, preparation, and trust. (Allsup, 2016)

These misgiving about the risk concept are understandable, but they may themselves be examples of an overprotective stance. We can distinguish between what is an adequate description of the phenomenon from a research perspective, where we seek to understand and find explanations to a phenomenon, and what sort of description might move parents to become less stressed and anxious about what might happen to their children if they get more freedom to roam. Critics of the concept of risky play may be right in saying that it is unlikely to sway overprotective parents into being more relaxed, since they already are worried about possible harm and injury to the children. Talk of risky play can have the effect of making them even more protective. However, when children climb trees, play with sharp knives, and go on solitary expeditions in their neighborhood these are in fact risky activities. These parents may be more comfortable with the softer language of adventurous and explorative play, but that may be because those concepts align well with their own need for control. Their children can explore and go on an adventure, but only under the supervising gaze of parents, or other qualified and responsible adults. By retaining the risk component in the language, we do not hide the fact that things might actually end badly. One significant dimension of risky play is that it can prepare children for dangerous and harmful circumstances, and also for failures, disappointments, and breakdowns in expectations. As will be argued later in the book, the real test of a commitment to allow risky play and risky work comes when things do actually end badly. We may theoretically accept that exposure to risk is good, in the upbringing of children as well as in nursing of elderly people, but be tempted to reconsider when a child or old person gets hurt.

2 Stoical Approaches

Stoicism is a philosophical tradition that has promoted the idea that human being can learn to meet hardship and difficulties with calm. It emerged in Cyprus around 300 B.C. and was a dominant feature in Hellenistic and Roman philosophy to around 300 A.C. The stoics taught that the path towards *eudaimonia* and a good life involved treating others with respect and fairness. Their philosophy was very much meant to be applied to everyday living. They argued that we should not let ourselves be controlled by cravings for pleasure or fear of pain, but use our reason to understand the world around us and participate with dignity in social life. At the core of this philosophy is the idea that human beings can train themselves not to be overwhelmed by strong emotions or pacified by previous experiences of failure and despair. Stoicism tells us that we can decide to look upon adversity as a source of learning, and shake off initial disappointments rather than dwell on our misfortune.

Stoicism has influenced philosophical reflections about what constitutes a good life for centuries. The three contemporary theoretical approaches discussed in this section have more or less loose relations to stoicism, in that they all explore ways in which children and adults alike can raise above adversity and learn from their participation in events where things have not gone according to plan. First, resilience addresses how individuals cope with adversity and are capable of bouncing back from negative experiences. An underlying idea is that the extent to which they have had the opportunity to engage in risky play can affect their level of resilience. Second, the distinction between a fixed and a growth mindset is useful for considering whether a person sees failure and lack of success in a particular endeavor as an opportunity for learning or not (Dweck, 2017). A person with a growth mindset will see the letdown as an opportunity to learn and prepare to do better next time, seeing his or her own capabilities as something fluid and formable, rather than fixed. Third, the distinction between understanding oneself primarily as an agent or a pawn, as an active initiator or a passive receiver of other people's instructions (Nygård, 2007), can shed light on the processes where people have to cope with their own and other people's fallibility at work.

Resilience has captured attention both in psychology and in organizational studies, and can shed light on the link between risky play and risky work. The concept has roots in the stoic tradition (Morris, 2004), in its depiction of how inner strength and calm can lead to outer achievements. One study indicates that resilience is different from stoicism in that it is flexible and action-oriented (Richardson & Chew-Graham, 2016), but that interpretation seems to be based on an oversight of the practical dimension of stoicism.

In the psychological research, resilience refers to a dynamic process encompassing positive adaptation within the context of significant adversity (Luthar et al., 2000, p. 543). Implicit within this notion are two critical conditions: (1) exposure to significant threat or severe adversity; and (2) the achievement of positive adaptation despite major assaults on the developmental process (Goldstein & Brooks, 2005; Masten et al., 1990). Resilience depicts the capacity to bounce back from negative experiences, and not be overwhelmed and pacified by setbacks. Individuals, groups, and organizations can be more or less resilient in the face of a struggle and imminent or real defeat. Systematic knowledge about the effects of risky play and the lack of it in childhood gives us reason to believe that building resilience on individual, group, and organizational levels depend on a societal acceptance and encouragement of risk-taking in childhood.

Resilience is often a factor in sports. One of the most memorable matches in the European Championships in football in 2016 provided a vivid example. An English national team consisting of star players from prestigious clubs like Manchester United, Liverpool, and Arsenal, faced an Icelandic team where the players came from much smaller, and lesser known, clubs in Sweden, Norway, and Wales. The match started predictably with an English goal, but the Icelandic team quickly responded by scoring two goals, and from there on controlled the game against the higher ranked and more famous opponents. Iceland looked more composed and alert, and knocked England out of the competition with a 2-1 win. On one interpretation, it was a match between a tough and resilient team, with a stoic ability to face a storm, and a weak group of superstars unprepared for struggle and fight. The English commentator

Jamie Carragher called it a generation problem, connected to upbringing and protection against taking misadventure personally:

> I call them the Academy Generation because they have come through in an era when footballers have never had more time being coached. (...) They get ferried to football schools, they work on immaculate pitches, play in pristine training gear every day and everything is done to ensure all they have to do is focus on football. We think we are making them men but actually we are creating babies. Life has been too easy. They have been pampered from a young age, had money thrown at them and, when things have gone wrong, they have been told it is never their fault. (Carragher, 2016)

On Carragher's interpretation, the English players were not ready for the toil of competing with the Icelandic team, because they had never become properly accustomed to hardship. Well-meaning parents and coaches had protected them against struggle, and thus inadvertently made them more or less incapacitated to bounce back and give another try. Their Icelandic opponents were individuals who from childhood had been used to cycle or walk through icy cold wind and rain to football practice, and had learned to look after themselves and take responsibility in stressful circumstances. The English team may have been superior in footballing technique and skills, but lacked the resilience and toughness to cope with the powerful Icelandic onslaught.

The second set of concepts that can help make sense of how risky play can prepare children for risky work is Dweck's distinction between *growth mindset* and *fixed mindset*. She describes her passage into the topic and the first realization that people differ in their approach to hardship in the following manner:

> I was obsessed with understanding how people cope with failures, and I decided to study it by watching how students grapple with hard problems. So I brought children one at the time to a room in their school, made them comfortable, and then gave them a series of puzzles to solve. The first ones were fairly easy, but the next ones were hard. As the students grunted, perspired, and toiled, I watched their strategies and probed what they were thinking and feeling.

Confronted with hard puzzles, one ten-year old boy pulled up his chair, rubbed his hands together, smacked his lips, and cried out "I love a challenge!" Another, sweating away on these puzzles, looked up with a pleased expression and said with authority, "You know, I was *hoping* this would be informative." (Dweck, 2017, p. 3)

These are the first encounters Dweck had with people she would later describe to have a growth mindset, who think that their capacities to solve problems and take on challenges can be cultivated and developed over time. The children she describes above, found thrill in the puzzles that seemed impossible to solve. They are different from people who see their intellectual and practical skills to be given, carved in stone, who have a fixed mindset. The former see failure as an opportunity to improve, while the latter see instances where they are unable to solve a problem or cope with a challenge as evidence of their own shortcomings.

On Dweck's interpretation, individuals with a fixed mindset believe that their intelligence and practical capabilities as simply inborn traits, and will tend to avoids situations where they may expose their own limitations. They value perceptions of smartness, and will attempt to cover up their weaknesses, since they perceive them to unchangeable. There is nothing to gain from encountering difficulties at the threshold of their given capacities, since they can end in embarrassment, when it becomes clear that they are not good enough to cope with challenges of that kind.

A person with a fixed mindset may believe that his or her given capacities are at an exceptionally high-level, as we will see in Chap. 5, in a narrative about high-ranking doctors who are reluctant to sit down with colleagues to analyze and discuss patient cases where complications have occurred, and outcomes have been worse than expected. On the initiative from doctors with a growth mindset, colleagues at a hospital unit meet regularly to talk about such cases. Of those who are attending, some believe that there is learning to be gained from carefully analyzing the cases on hindsight, and considering what they as professionals could and should have done differently, while others tend to explain mishaps and unforeseen complications as a result of bad luck, and not something they could have influenced by doing a better job. In terms of the temporal structure of past, present, and future, the doctors who are willing to scrutinize their contribution at a critical event now, seem to increase their chances of doing a high-quality professional service to their patients later. Those who are not, demonstrate a fixed mindset that can pose a threat to patient safety. This example will be elaborated and discussed more fully in Chap. 5.

In her research, Dweck has found that it is possible to foster and develop growth mindset through feedback strategies. Praise and encouragement for concrete effort and persistence can help children to learn and adopt effective strategies for learning. A range of studies document that growth mindset makes a positive difference in student and adult achievement, both short-term and long-term (Schroder et al., 2017a, 2017b; Yeager et al., 2016).

The third set of concepts that can illuminate the relation between risky play and risky work is the distinction between agent and pawn as alternative modes of self-understanding (Nygård, 2007). During childhood and upbringing, we build up mental resources to face the changing realities of adulthood. One noteworthy dimension of that development is the kind of self-understanding we develop and normalize. To what extent do we see ourselves primarily as active and responsible individuals, with opportunities to influence the directions our lives take, and to what extent do we see ourselves mainly as passive recipients of input from others? Agents and pawns differ in how they view their scope of action and responsibility for taking initiatives in the situations they face (Table 1).

Table 1 Self-understanding

Agent	Pawn
• My scope of action is large, and in considerable degree defined by me • I take initiatives and do not await instructions • It is my responsibility to find solutions and decide what to do	• My scope of action is small, and in considerable degree defined by others • I do not take initiatives, but await instructions from others • It is other people's responsibility to find solutions and decide what to do

The parenting regimes children grow up under are likely to affect the extent to which they come to understand themselves primarily as agents or pawns. Those who become used to having the freedom to explore and expand their own scope of action are more likely to develop an agent-understanding, while those who experience stricter adult supervision, become used to seeing themselves more as pawns. Similar patterns of self-understanding and behavior have been studied under the heading of locus of control, focusing on the extent to which people perceive that they are in charge of the events in their lives (Hou, Doerr, Johnson, & Chen, 2017).

People apparently do not see themselves consistently as either agents or pawns, but tend to move between these two poles of self-understanding, using agent-language in describing their activities and roles in one setting, and pawn-language in another. Simple and seemingly innocuous statements about our own contribution to a state of affairs can reveal our current self-understanding. "I did not get time" is a typical pawn-statement, indicating that time is a commodity handed out by others, and not something that the person has control over. A parallel agent-statement can be "I did not prioritize it" or "I decided not to spend time on it". Consider a young man who for a long time has been without a job, and lived on unemployment benefit. He has developed anger towards the employment authorities. "Now they have turned me into a thief", he says. When asked to explain how, and he claims that the unemployment support had not arrived on the due date, and he had run out of food. His only alternative, as he saw it, had been to go to the local grocery store and steal something to eat. In his account of this turn of events, there had been no real alternatives to stealing food, and he felt genuinely forced by the authorities to become a thief. His scope of action was small and tight, and defined by others. He sees himself to be a pawn, and not an agent. When pressed to take at least some responsibility for his actions in the grocery store, he refuses to do that, and remains in pawn-mode. When we see ourselves as pawns, we interpret events in the world as that which merely happens to us, while in agent-mode, we acknowledge responsibility for our contributions to how things turn out.

Attribution theory sheds further light on how we take responsibility or not for events connected to our own decisions and behavior (Weiner, 1972). It focuses on how we explain outcomes in terms of internal or external factors, or what has been within or outside our own control. To take another example from football, one Norwegian coach famously claimed after his underdog team had won the cup final that "this was world class coaching", thus placing himself in the center of attention, as the agents who had made the right decisions to overcome a higher ranked opponent (Rekdal, 2009). The same coach has a tendency, when his team loses, to blame external circumstances like the referee or the lack commitment from his players, for the outcome. When his team wins, he tends to see himself as an agent, while a loss triggers a pawn mentality.

Outcomes in a range of situations depend crucially on whether people see themselves as agents or pawns. These self-understandings affect decision-making and conduct in critical situations, when something out of the ordinary happens. We can think back on the example in the introduction, involving the driver of the push-back tractor at the airport. His intervention and continued insistence that the dripping from the wing should be checked properly before takeoff is typical agent-behavior. It was not part of his job instruction to be in dialog with the people in the cockpit about that issue. He could have made his observation once, and left the further decision-making to the pilot and co-pilot, but instead continued to voice his concern. In doing so, he took responsibility beyond his formal job description. Similar situations occur in other workplaces, and outcomes often crucially depend on whether people see themselves primarily as agents or pawns. A range of psychological factors can influence self-understanding and personal confidence in such situations, as will be discussed in the coming chapters. The main purpose here has been to highlight the distinction between two polarized ways of seeing one's own role and responsibilities. It is likely that upbringing and parenting influences whether children primarily develop agent—or pawn-understandings of themselves, and that risky play can be crucial in teaching them to explore actively their own scope of action.

The main line of thinking in this chapter has been that risky play during childhood can prepare individuals for active participation in risky endeavors at work. When children get the freedom to roam and explore their environment below the adults' radar, they can develop the autonomy and confidence they need to engage in risky work when they grow older. The anti-phobic effects of risky play can make the children more robust and resilient, and prepare them for an adult life where they

Table 2 Adversity time frame

Before	Critical quality moment	After
Risky play can create • Resilience • Growth mindset • Agent understanding of self	A challenging event that turns into an unwelcome and unpleasant experience	• I will bounce back • I can learn from this • It is up to me to bounce back and learn

are likely to encounter significant adversity in organizational settings. We can place the preparation for, the experience of, and responses to critical events in a threefold temporal frame of what happens before, during, and after it takes place (Table 2).

Childhood research indicates that overprotective parents and authorities pose an obstacle to healthy developments when they put restrictions on the children's scope of action. The intention may be to put the children's safety first, but one unintended outcome appears to be that their mental and physical development suffers. Risky play can crucially make the children aware of their own fallibility, and provides them with opportunities to learn to cope with their own and other people's tendencies to make mistakes. When dramatic slips and blunders happen at work, they may not be overwhelmed and pacified by it, since they are used to such events from childhood. Initiatives to develop free-range kids should be encouraged from organizations, since, in the long-term, those are the people who are likely to be best prepared for the challenges of adult working life, through a growth mindset and through resilience. It is also through this kind of upbringing that children can learn to see themselves primarily as autonomous and responsible agents, and not as pawns that are moved around by forces beyond their own control.

References

Adams, J. (2001). *Risk*. London: Routledge.
Allsup, K. (2016). Please don't say you allow your child to take risks. Retrieved from https://childrengrowing.com/2016/06/08/please-dont-say-you-allow-your-child-to-take-risks/.
Ball, D. J. (2002). *Playgrounds-risks, benefits and choices*. London: HSE Books.
Bjorklund, D. F., & Pellegrini, A. D. (2000). Child development and evolutionary psychology. *Child Development, 71*(6), 1687–1708.

Bjorklund, D. F., & Pellegrini, A. D. (2002). *The origins of human nature: Evolutionary developmental psychology*. American Psychological Association.

Byers, J. A., & Walker, C. (1995). Refining the motor training hypothesis for the evolution of play. *The American Naturalist, 146*(1), 25–40.

Carragher, J. (2016, 28 June). English players are weak. *Daily Mail*. Retrieved from http://www.dailymail.co.uk/sport/article-3664847/JAMIE-CARRAGHER-S-DAMNING-VERDICT-English-players-weak-think-making-men-creating-babies.html.

Cevher-Kalburan, N., & Ivrendi, A. (2016). Risky play and parenting styles. *Journal of Child and Family Studies, 25*(2), 355–366.

Clements, R. (2004). An investigation of the status of outdoor play. *Contemporary Issues in Early Childhood, 5*(1), 68–80.

DiLillo, D., Potts, R., & Himes, S. (1998). Predictors of children's risk appraisals. *Journal of Applied Developmental Psychology, 19*(3), 415–427.

Dweck, C. (2017). *Mindset: Changing the way you think to fulfill your potential*. London: Hachette UK.

Francis, M., & Lorenzo, R. (2006). Children and city design: Proactive process and the 'renewal' of childhood. In C. Spencer & M. Blades (Eds.), *Children and their environments: Learning, using and designing spaces* (pp. 217–237). Cambridge: Cambridge University Press.

Goldstein, S., & Brooks, R. B. (2005). *Resilience in children*. New York: Springer.

Greve, W., Thomsen, T., & Dehio, C. (2014). Does playing pay? The fitness-effect of free play during childhood. *Evolutionary Psychology, 12*(2).

Hou, N., Doerr, A., Johnson, B. A., & Chen, P. Y. (2017). *Locus of control the handbook of stress and health: A guide to research and practice* (p. 283). Hoboken, NJ: Wiley.

Lavrysen, A., Bertrands, E., Leyssen, L., Smets, L., Vanderspikken, A., & De Graef, P. (2017). Risky-play at school. Facilitating risk perception and competence in young children. *European Early Childhood Education Research Journal, 25*(1), 89–105.

Luthar, S. S., Cicchetti, D., & Becker, B. (2000). The construct of resilience: A critical evaluation and guidelines for future work. *Child Development, 71*(3), 543–562.

Masten, A. S., Best, K. M., & Garmezy, N. (1990). Resilience and development: Contributions from the study of children who overcome adversity. *Development and Psychopathology, 2*(04), 425–444.

Morris, T. V. (2004). *The stoic art of living: Inner resilience and outer results*. Chicago, Illinois: Open Court Publishing.
Nygård, R. (2007). *Aktør eller brikke: Søkelys på menneskers selvforståelse*. Oslo: Cappelen Damm.
Oxford living dictionaries. (2017). Oxford: Oxford University Press.
Pellegrini, A. D., & Smith, P. K. (1998). Physical activity play: The nature and function of a neglected aspect of play. *Child Development, 69*(3), 577–598.
Plumert, J. M. (1995). Relations between children's overestimation of their physical abilities and accident proneness. *Developmental Psychology, 31*(5), 866.
Plumert, J. M., & Schwebel, D. C. (1997). Social and temperamental influences on children's overestimation of their physical abilities: Links to accidental injuries. *Journal of Experimental Child Psychology, 67*(3), 317–337.
Poulton, R., Davies, S., Menzies, R. G., Langley, J. D., & Silva, P. A. (1998). Evidence for a non-associative model of the acquisition of a fear of heights. *Behaviour Research and Therapy, 36*(5), 537–544.
Rakison, D. H. (2005). Developing knowledge of objects' motion properties in infancy. *Cognition, 96*(3), 183–214.
Rekdal, K. (2009, 8th November) *Coaching i verdensklasse/Interviewer: A. Borge*. TV2 Norway.
Richardson, J. C., & Chew-Graham, C. A. (2016). Resilience and well-being. In *Mental Health and Older People* (pp. 9–17). Springer.
Sandseter, E. B. H. (2007a). Categorising risky play—How can we identify risk-taking in children's play? *European Early Childhood Education Research Journal, 15*(2), 237–252.
Sandseter, E. B. H. (2007b). Risky play among four-and five-year-old children in preschool. In O'Brien, S., Cassidy, P., & Shonfeld, H (Eds.), *Vision into practice: Making quality a reality in the lives of young children* (pp. 248–256). Dublin: CECDE.
Sandseter, E. B. H., & Kennair, L. E. O. (2011). Children's risky play from an evolutionary perspective: The anti-phobic effects of thrilling experiences. *Evolutionary Psychology, 9*(2), 257–284.
Sandseter, E. B. H., & Sando, O. J. (2016). "We don't allow children to climb trees": How a focus on safety affects Norwegian children's play in early-childhood education and care settings. *American Journal of Play, 8*(2), 178.
Schroder, H. S., Fisher, M. E., Lin, Y., Lo, S. L., Danovitch, J. H., & Moser, J. S. (2017a). Neural evidence for enhanced attention to mistakes among

school-aged children with a growth mindset. *Developmental Cognitive Neuroscience, 24,* 42–50.

Schroder, H. S., Yalch, M. M., Dawood, S., Callahan, C. P., Donnellan, M. B., & Moser, J. S. (2017b). Growth mindset of anxiety buffers the link between stressful life events and psychological distress and coping strategies. *Personality and Individual Differences, 110,* 23–26.

Skenazy, L. (2008, 1st April). Why I let my 9 year old ride the subway alone, commentary. *New York Sun.* Retrieved from http://www.nysun.com/opinion/why-i-let-my-9-year-old-ride-subway-alone/73976/.

Voce, A. (2016). The trouble with risky play. Retrieved from https://policyforplay.com/2016/06/08/the-trouble-with-risky-play/?fb_action_ids=10154040579166609&fb_action_types=news.publishes.

Webpage for Bsafe. Retrieved from http://getbsafe.com/.

Weiner, B. (1972). Theories of motivation: From mechanism to cognition.

Yeager, D. S., Romero, C., Paunesku, D., Hulleman, C. S., Schneider, B., Hinojosa, C., ... Roberts, A. (2016). Using design thinking to improve psychological interventions: The case of the growth mindset during the transition to high school. *Journal of Educational Psychology, 108*(3), 374.

Open Access This chapter is licensed under the terms of the Creative Commons Attribution 4.0 International License (http://creativecommons.org/licenses/by/4.0/), which permits use, sharing, adaptation, distribution and reproduction in any medium or format, as long as you give appropriate credit to the original author(s) and the source, provide a link to the Creative Commons license and indicate if changes were made.

The images or other third party material in this chapter are included in the chapter's Creative Commons license, unless indicated otherwise in a credit line to the material. If material is not included in the chapter's Creative Commons license and your intended use is not permitted by statutory regulation or exceeds the permitted use, you will need to obtain permission directly from the copyright holder.

2
Failing Fast

Inga Bolstad is the director general of the National Archives of Norway. In Spring 2016, she made the decision to terminate a complex and prestigious development project. Considerable resources had been invested to create a common platform for archiving documents for the Norwegian public sector. The overall aim of the project had been to counter what Bolstad calls digital dementia, the forgetting of vital public information regarding taxation, health, education, and other kinds of services offered to citizens and organizations in society. Norway needed an electronic archive for local and central public administrations, and the E-archive Project was supposed to provide it. "The time horizon for such a project is, if not eternity, at least a thousand years. Our nation's common memory depends on a well-functioning digital depot. The stability of our democratic system relies on easy electronic access to documents from the past, and it is our responsibility to build it" (Bolstad, 2017). Stakes were thus high to come up with a robust and reliable solution, but the first attempt failed.

"We took the decision to terminate the project after a meeting with the Digitalization Council, the government appointed unit set up to give advice to public organizations about digital projects. The Council provided constructive criticism regarding what we had done so far and the plans for the further development of the project. Now we realized that it had been wrong to go for one particular alternative from the beginning of the project, since it had made us lose sight of other viable alternatives. Furthermore, we had primarily focused on our own needs and goals, and not taken sufficiently into account those of the people who were supposed to use the system on a daily basis. There was also a lack of properly defined milestones for the project, where we could have taken the temperature on the development and progress. When I entered a meeting with twelve people currently working on the project, and asked them about its purpose and direction, I got twelve significantly different answers. All of this made us understand that the E-archive project was about to become a fiasco, and we decided to stop it. We had failed, and realized that it was best to take a step back and start afresh" (Bolstad, 2017).

The topic of this chapter is the role of failure in innovative processes. A range of studies has focused on experimentation and how organizational structures and incentives should encourage it (Ahuja & Lampert, 2001; Cannon & Edmondson, 2005; Lee, Edmondson, Thomke, & Worline, 2004). With active experimentation comes the risk of failure, and leaders in organizations tend to be reluctant to talk about it, because they assume that failure is bad. That is often a misguided assumption, since failure is an integral part of testing hypotheses about the world, and in experimental explorations to develop new products and services (Edmondson, 2011). Narratives about failure can also be sources of significant organizational learning (Bledow, Carette, Kühnel, & Bister, 2017; Rami & Gould, 2016; Shepherd, Patzelt, & Wolfe, 2011).

When a pilot or a surgeon makes a mistake, it can lead to truly bad and devastating outcomes, but in other organizational settings, to fail can often be a welcome dimension of learning and development. In innovation, "failing fast" has become a viable catchword, indicating that individuals, groups, and organizations should stop wasting valuable time and resources by remaining loyal to one particular idea. The successful design company IDEO's slogan is "Fail often in order to succeed sooner," and other companies are attempting to adopt a similar stance in order to reduce the stigma of failure (Edmondson, 2011).

This chapter explores how learning from failure requires close attention to the distinction between causes of failure and blame for failure. It also identifies and discusses three psychological phenomena that pose a challenge to effective learning from failure. All of them have links to the communication climate for voicing a concern that the proposed course of action may not after all be the best one. First, *the sunk-cost-fallacy* is the tendency we have to follow through on an activity even when it is not meeting our expectations, because of the resources we have already invested in it. Second, research on *the bystander effect* indicates that the more people who are witness to an event that calls for help or some other form of intervention, the less likely it is that anybody will step forward and help or intervene. Third, people are vulnerable to *the confirmation fallacy*, in that they have a tendency to notice information that is in line with their beliefs and assumptions, and to disregard information that gives them reason to reconsider. These three phenomena are well documented and known from social psychology, and the aim here is to connect them to challenges regarding fallibility at work. The context in the current chapter is that of innovation and the need to fail fast, but an understanding of the three psychological phenomena is also relevant in situations where it is urgent to speak up about mistakes because they can lead to harm, as in aviation and healthcare, as will be demonstrated in coming chapters.

1 Innovation and Failure

In the aftermath of the termination of E-archive, Bolstad and her organization have received positive responses on the decision, and on the willingness to share the narrative of their failure. The Agency for Public Management and eGovernment in Norway has an annual conference for dwelling on mistakes in the public sector, called Feiltrinn (Misstep). The idea behind it is to create a learning platform for public organizations who are dealing with similarly complex projects as E-archive, and need to identify and learn from mistakes. In December 2016, Bolstad took the stage at the conference to talk about the mistakes in the E-archive project, and how they had affected her organization. Her narrative of failure was highly relevant for the other participants, several of whom worked on other digital projects in the public sector, and could easily end up in similar circumstances of having to decide whether to stop a project and admit failure, or not.

Bolstad has highlighted the learning aspect of the closing down the E-project. "We have failed, but the experience made us stronger. We are now an organization where it is acceptable to try, fail, learn, and move on. One other notable thing is that have become more professional in handling disagreement. That is a prerequisite for open and honest talk about our projects" (Bolstad, 2017). The need to create a digital depot for the public sector in Norway remains, and the current efforts to do so are different from the first in four significant dimensions, in that the project is characterized by:

- Stronger user orientation, taking into account the needs and competencies of the people who are going to use the system.
- Not just one, but multiple alternatives for a solution are under consideration from the start.
- A communication climate where people are encouraged to voice concerns and disagreements early.
- Tolerance for failure in the process of developing the alternatives.

What Bolstad describes as the key elements in the work to counter digital dementia overlaps with the main tenets of design thinking, where principles of design are applied to the way people work. This approach focuses on users' experiences in encounters with technologically complex processes and uses prototypes to explore potential solutions. It is built on the assumption that some alternatives need to fail in order for others to stand out as the better ones. Design thinking has proved to be especially useful in addressing wicked problems (Buchanan, 1992), that is, problems with high levels of complexity and ambiguity. A common aim for such processes is to make the users' interaction with the technological solutions intuitive and pleasurable. That is the task for the team currently working in Bolstad's organization to create a digital archive. At the time of the interview, they had seven active conceptual alternatives, and will eventually converge on one of them for further development and implementation. One of the alternatives was similar to the original and discarded project, but now it was measured up against a range of other viable options.

Toleration for failure is a dimension of innovative work, since it is rare to get things right the first time (Kolko, 2015), as experienced by Bolstad and her team. In some contexts, what counts as getting things right is quite clearly defined and well understood, while in others, the process may lead to unexpected breakthroughs outside the scope of the original project. Here are four examples of what has been labeled accidental innovation (Austin, Devin, & Sullivan, 2012):

> 3M attempted to create a super-adhesive that could be used in the construction of planes, and instead ended up with a weak adhesive that was labelled "a solution without a problem". Employee Arthur Fry heard about the failure, and noticed that pieces of paper with the weak adhesive could be used as bookmarks, since they could be reused and could be peeled away without leaving any marks on the pages. Fry applied for a grant to develop the idea further, and the failed attempt to make super-glue led to the development of the Post-it note. (Brand, 1998; Govindarajan & Srinivas, 2013)
>
> The drug Sildenafil Nitrate was originally intended as a treatment for angina, but turned out to be ineffective for that purpose. Nurses participating in the testing of the drug noted that the patients who took the drug got penile erections. Their copious notes of side effects from the trails led to the discovery of Viagra. A failure to develop a drug to treat chest pains thus became a successful drug to treat erection problems. (Cook, 2016)
>
> The Norwegian company Tine tried to develop and manufacture a salami sausage made from salmon. It failed, because the customers and market did not show any interest in the salmon salami. The failed sausage was based on the use of new fermentation technology that made it possible to send exceptionally fresh filets of salmon to the market. The raw material to be used in the sausage had to be of exceptional quality for the technology to work. The company got this from a salmon provider that had developed a technology to distribute fresh fish to the market immediately after the fileting process had taken place. The commercial director realized that it was much easier to sell the raw material (the exceptionally fresh salmon filets) than the salami itself. This product was called Salma,

a name originally designed for the failed salmon salami sausage, and it turned out to become a great commercial success. (Hoholm, 2011)

One late evening at the restaurant Osteria Francescana, a three-Michelin-star restaurant in Modena, Italy, the sous chef prepared the last dessert dish, a lemon tart. On his way out of the kitchen to the guests' table he dropped the plate, half of the tart ended up on the counter, and half remained on the plate. The sous chef despaired, but the master chef Massimo Bottura saw it as on opportunity to create a new dish. Together they rearranged the lemon tart on the plate, and served it as if the destructed tart was according to plan, calling the dish "Ooops! I dropped the lemon tart". It has since become a signature dish in the restaurant. (Gelb, 2015)

The first, second, and third examples are of innovation processes that accidentally led to the discovery of a different product to that envisaged by the initiators. The fourth is not an innovation process as such, but rather an accident in the implementation of a creative process. What the four examples have in common is that somebody had an eye for possibilities and were able to turn failure into a surprising success.

2 Beyond Blame

After more than two decades of studying failure, Edmondson (2011) has noted that executives and managers tend to think about it in the wrong way. She believes that the main reason why they struggle to do so that they are trapped in a false dichotomy: "How can you respond constructively to failures without giving rise to an anything goes attitude? If people aren't blamed for failures, what will ensure that they try as hard as possible to do their best work?" (Edmondson, 2011, p. 50). Managers seem to believe that they have to blame and criticize employees who fail, because otherwise they will become complacent and think that it does not really matter whether they do the best they can at work.

In order to disentangle this dichotomy, Edmondson goes on to provide a spectrum of reasons for failure, ranging from deliberative deviations at one end, to exploratory testing at the other. An act of choosing to violate a process or procedure tends to be blameworthy, as when a flight crew skips parts of procedures before takeoff, or a doctor fails to wash his or her hands properly before treating a patient. These are unwelcome occurrences, and if the manager does not intervene to blame the responsible individuals, it may indeed lead to complacency and an anything goes attitude.

The situation is very different on the other side of the scale, where the aim is to expand knowledge and generate solutions by testing out ideas, to see if they are worth pursuing. Here, a failure can be a welcome event, something that enables the group or organization to move forward with the knowledge that this particular idea did not work. The decision to stop e-Archive and start afresh with new ideas can serve as an example of such an event. In the beginning, it can be painful to accept failure, in light of so many hours and so much energy spent to get things right. Gradually that feeling may give way to relief at being able to pursue new directions. Any manager who fails to see the difference between mistakes on opposite sides of the spectrum outlined by Edmondson and blames employees when things go wrong during experimentation or hypothesis testing is likely to hamper innovation.

In between the two endpoints of deviance and exploratory testing lie the reasons for failure where it is more difficult to attribute degrees of blame. The root cause of why things go wrong may be that the agent is inattentive, lacks ability, or has been given faulty or incomplete instructions about how to act. It can happen in a hospital, when inexperienced doctors or nurses get tasks that are at the limits of their current competence. When things go wrong, and patients are harmed, it can be difficult to establish whether the cause is primarily a personal mistake on the part of the doctor or nurse, or a systemic mistake, as when the person should have received better training, instruction, and support from seniors. In such cases, the blame may partly lie with the executive or managers who have put the person in that position and partly with the person him or herself, who should have spoken up about competence limitations. One concrete way to respond when facing a situation where personal competence is stretched is to ask for help, a topic explored further in Chap. 6 . The main reason for failure may also be that the task itself is difficult, or that the situation is complex and ambiguous. The more the failure can be adequately accounted for by appeal to circumstances, the less room remains for reasonable blame.

Edmondson warns leaders and other decision-makers against entering a blame game in the aftermath of a bad outcome. Many failures in organizations are not truly blameworthy, and when they are mistreated as such, it is likely to block learning. Collins (2001) used the term "autopsy without blame" to establish a similar thought. In situations where things do not go well, the organization can analyze them and try to figure out what happened, without attributing blame. Learning and development depend on cool heads that keep any tendency towards blame and punishment at bay, at least during the analyzing phase. In some cases, the result of the inquiry into the causes of the failure may be that some people are actually to blame and are not fit to perform the kind of task in question. That conclusion, however, should come at the end of careful reflection about the probable causes, all through the spectrum of reasons for failure Edmondson outlines.

The attitude of performing an autopsy without blame can be crucial when interviewing people about their own behavior and that of their colleagues in events leading up to an accident. Whether the interviewer focuses on (i) causes or (ii) blame is likely to affect the openness of the interviewee. If the latter senses that (ii) is the prime perspective, answers tend to become more defensive and weighted, and the likelihood decreases of getting a full and honest account of events at hand. In aviation, autopsy without blame has become common practice and has contributed to improved safety (Stoop & Kahan, 2005), while in healthcare, a blame focus has been documented to inhibit reporting of medical failure (Bond, 2008; Waring, 2005). Lessons from aviation on dealing with fallibility and blame to strengthen safety have received increasing interest in healthcare and medicine. Chapters 4 and 5 in this book will explore in further detail alternative approaches to fallibility at work in both these sectors of organizational life.

3   Three Obstacles

Learning from failure requires that missteps are detected and brought to the surface. In organizational settings, whether that happens or not depends on the communication climate, and particularly on the extent to which it is normal for employees to speak up when they sense that something is wrong with a project or initiative. The climate and the individuals who operate in it are put to the test in critical quality moments, situations where the next thing to happen determine whether events unfold in a positive or negative manner. Research in social psychology has identified cognitive biases that tend to hamper our abilities to act rationally in concrete circumstances. Three of them are particularly relevant in the context of voicing concerns about failures and mistakes. First, *the sunk-cost fallacy* is the tendency we have to remain committed to a decision or plan, even when we know that they are not living up to expectations. Second, *the bystander effect* indicates that the more people who are witnesses to a failure and can intervene, the less is the likelihood that anybody will actually make an intervention. Third, *the confirmation fallacy* makes us stick to initial assumptions and beliefs about states of affairs, and overlook information that gives us reason to revise them.

In decision-making and economics, a sunk cost is a cost that has already been incurred and cannot be recovered (Kahneman & Tversky, 1979). From a perspective of rational decision-making, sunk cost should not affect current decisions about how to go forward, since whatever the decision-maker does from now on will not change the fact of that cost. Only prospective costs should be taken into consideration. In reality, sunk costs do influence decision-making and can make people pursue projects and plans that are not living up to expectations, or are not in line with their current priorities (Fischer, Greitemeyer, Pollozek, & Frey, 2006; Friedman, Pommerenke, Lukose, Milam, & Huberman, 2007). The sunk-cost fallacy is sometimes also named as the Concorde fallacy, after the escalating and expensive efforts to make a success of that supersonic airplane (Arkes & Ayton, 1999).

Research on the sunk-cost fallacy has identified two psychological explanations for the bias. One is that information about failure creates cognitive dissonance (Gilad, Kaish, & Loeb, 1987; Staw, 1976). We want to believe that the initial decision was rational and correct, and now face information to the contrary. One way to reduce the mental discomfort of cognitive dissonance is to strengthen the belief in the decision to go ahead. Self-justification can take the form of continuing to add resources to a project, thus keeping the discomfort at bay, and prolonging a bad project. We can agree with the saying that if you have dug yourself into a hole, you should stop digging, but in reality, we struggle to live in accordance with that claim. The commitment to pour further resources into the project appears to be stronger the more personally responsible the decision-maker takes him- or herself to be for the initial decision to start (Bazerman, Giuliano, & Appelman, 1984; Staw, 1976).

The second explanation for the sunk-cost bias is loss aversion, or misgivings about wasting resources (Kahneman & Tversky, 1979). When a person has bought a non-refundable ticket for a theatre show and finds on the evening of the show that another way to spend the evening appears much more attractive, the sunk-cost fallacy can make that person decide to go to the theatre show after all, in order not to have wasted money on the ticket. Economists will claim that the person has the choice between double and single suffering, that is (1) the suffering of having paid for the ticket and the suffering of a suboptimal evening at the theatre, and (2) the suffering of having paid for the ticket and the pleasure of a better evening away from the theatre. Of these options, (2) is clearly the more rational, but in real life we can see a tendency to choose (1) (Arkes & Blumer, 1985).

Bolstad's decision to terminate the E-archive project can be seen as a successful effort to overcome the sunk-cost fallacy. Considerable resources had already been invested in the project, and a decision to stop it would reflect badly on those who decided to go ahead with it. The first explanation of sunk-cost fallacy indicates that Bolstad and her top management team may have been inclined to continue the project, to keep the cognitive dissonance of admitting a previous mistake at bay. Furthermore, they faced a voice between (1) the suffering of having spent time and money on a failed project coupled with the suffering of failing to create a well-functioning digital depot and (2) the same suffering of having used resources on a failed project, coupled with an opportunity to pursue new initiatives, better designed for the purpose of delivering a functional digital archive for the Norwegian public sector.

The bystander effect is another psychological phenomenon that can stand in the way of effective communication about actual and immerging failures. Studies show that the presence of other people in a critical situation reduces the likelihood that a person will help. The more people who are present as bystanders, the less likely that the person will take an initiative to help (Fischer et al., 2011; Latané, 1981; Latané & Darley, 1976; Latané & Nida, 1981). It has also been documented that people do not have to be physically present in order for bystander effects to occur, as it can also affect interactions on the internet (Barron & Yechiam, 2002; Blair, Thompson, & Wuensch, 2005). The phenomenon is alluded to in explanations of social networking (Chiu & Chang, 2015) and the effectiveness of loyalty program marketing (Steinhoff & Palmatier, 2016). Bystander effects can also occur among small children (Plötner, Over, Carpenter, & Tomasello, 2015).

It has not been empirically tested whether bystander effects can occur in organizational setting where employees are aware of weaknesses or mistakes in projects, but findings in other areas of research make it plausible that even in such contexts, the likelihood that anybody will intervene to help in a project crisis can be affected by the size of the group of bystanders. The two main explanations of the bystander effect probably transfer over to organizational settings. First, diffusion of responsibility is the tendency we have to attribute individual responsibility based on the number of people who are present (Darley & Latané, 1968). We tend to see a responsibility to intervene and do something as one particular entity, shared evenly and fairly among the people who are present. According to this line of thinking, if we are 100 people present, we each have roughly 1/100 responsibility to do something. That is a very tiny piece of responsibility, and each of us can move away from the situation without having done anything, without a bad conscience. If we are 50 people present, that gives each of us about 1/50 responsibility to intervene, which is twice as much as in the first scenario, but still only a minimal amount of responsibility. The moral reasoning behind diffusion of responsibility is flawed (Parfit, 1984). It seems reasonable to attribute responsibility more on the basis of what each individual is capable of doing, and give less weight to the number of people present. Despite philosophical arguments to the contrary, however, diffusion of responsibility is a common and stable feature in human behavior.

The second cause of the bystander effect is the well-documented phenomenon of pluralistic ignorance, the tendency we have to adjust and correct our own judgement of the situation at hand, in light of what we take to be other people's judgements of it (Beu, Buckley, & Harvey, 2000; Zhu & Westphal, 2011). A person may initially believe that the individuals in front of him or her need help. If a crowd of other people are behaving as if that is not the case, the person can mistakenly assume that (i) he or she is the only one present who believes that those individuals need help and (ii) that the initial belief is false. A bystander effect can occur in a real and acute crisis when individuals start to doubt their own judgement due to the passivity of the people around them. Initial alarm at seeing other people in distress can vanish at the sight of a calm crowd.

It is possible to imagine similar processes in organizations, when initially promising ideas and plans turn out to have significant weaknesses. Bystander effects can put the detection of failure in a project on hold. First, a large group of people may have access to the relevant information, but diffusion of responsibility can set in and make each of them believe that they only have a microscopic responsibility for voicing their concern, given the considerable size of the group that has the same information. Second, pluralistic ignorance can make each of those who have doubts about the project adjust their judgement because nobody else shows any signs of questioning the quality of the project. These two phenomena in tandem can cause a bystander effect, and thus a continuation of projects that should have been identified as failures.

Even though the bystander effect lacks a reasonable foundation, it poses a challenge in organizational contexts where it is important to detect failure quickly and forcefully. One way to neutralize it can be to address individuals one by one and ask them for feedback about the particular project. If the project owner asks 100 people simultaneously about their beliefs about the current state of the project, face-to-face in an auditorium or through digital media, each them are likely to assume that they only have 1/100 responsibility to respond. In order to overcome that effect, the project owner can address one individual at the time, and invite a response. That places the task of responding firmly in the lap of one individual and preempts diffusion of responsibility. A move of this kind is also likely to puncture pluralistic ignorance, since the respondent is now invited to express his or her personal beliefs, and not those of the entire group. The move of addressing one respondent at the time does not guarantee that the feedback has high quality, but at least it appears to be an effective way of neutralizing the bystander effect.

The third psychological phenomenon that can affect identification of failure is confirmation fallacy. People tend to notice information that confirms their current beliefs, and disregard information that provides them with reasons to reconsider those beliefs (Hart et al., 2009; Nickerson, 1998; Shefrin, 2007). Perception psychology has identified one particular way that the confirmation fallacy can set in, focusing on the assumption that in order to see something, one simply needs to direct one's eyes toward it. Simons and Chabris (1999) have challenged that assumption, most notably through their so-called gorilla experiment. In that experiment, an audience watches a short film, where three people in white clothes and three people in black clothes walk around on a small area, passing basketballs to each other. The task for the audience is to count the number of times the white team manages to pass the ball to each other, while they ignore what the black team is doing. After seeing the film, the audience is asked whether they noticed anything else happening in it. Some people claim to have seen a black figure walking across the playing field. When watching the film for the second time, now without the task of counting passes, everybody can see that a person dressed up as a gorilla walks slowly into the frame, stops in the middle of it, bangs his or her chest, and walks slowly out again. The gorilla is big, and people who do not see it the first time are amazed and surprised that they could fail to do so. Kahneman (2010, p. 24) has noted how the gorilla experiment illustrates the double nature of this blindness: "We can be blind to the obvious, and we are also blind to our blindness." The research label for the phenomenon is inattentional blindness (Kreitz, Furley, Memmert, & Simons, 2016; Mack, 2003; Simons & Chabris, 1999).

In an organizational context, the people involved can have fixed beliefs about the quality of a project or idea and about the competence of the people involved in realizing it and overlook information that gives them reason to reconsider. The beliefs may be more optimistic and positive than the available information gives a foundation for, but also more pessimistic and negative. Looking back on examples from the current chapter, the confirmation fallacy can stand in the way of realizing that:

- What appears to be a good idea is actually a failure (E-Archive).
- What appears to be a failure is actually a good idea (Post-It/Viagra/Bottora's lemon tart).

There can be similar challenges with regard to taking in information about the competence and behavior of people who have a particular status in their professional environments:

- A person who has the status of being an expert is actually making or proposing a mistake.
- A person who has the status of being not that good is actually doing or proposing the right thing.

In order to overcome the confirmation fallacy, it can be necessary to invite other people to look at the situation and inquire about their perceptions of it. Research and experience provide emphatic evidence of how powerful and pervasive the fallacy is, and how dependent we are at individual, group, and organizational levels on a communication climate where people speak up when they notice events and occurrences out of the ordinary.

This chapter has focused on the role of failure in innovative processes. Failure is an integral part of testing hypotheses and ideas about how things work, and in competitive contexts, it can be crucial to be able to fail fast. However, the stigma of failure can be present in many organizational contexts, leading to continuation of projects that should have been terminated. The National Archives of Norway managed to break the stigma and stop the first attempt to develop a comprehensive digital depot for the public sector. In the process of doing so, they more or less explicitly overcame three psychological obstacles to learning from mistakes, in that they were not derailed by (i) the sunk-cost fallacy, (ii) the bystander effect, or (iii) the confirmation fallacy. They were also able to avoid the kind of blame-game that often characterizes the periods after an organization has experienced failure. The coming chapters will discuss examples from other organizational settings, where the ambition may be different from innovative processes, but the obstacles to detecting failure and voicing concern are similar. Even in those contexts, individuals can be blind to important aspects of their work, and blind to that blindness. They depend upon colleagues or other individuals in their proximity to speak up and intervene in critical quality moments, the situations where what happens next will determine whether things turn out well, nor not.

References

Ahuja, G., & Lampert, C. M. (2001). Entrepreneurship in the large corporation: A longitudinal study of how established firms create breakthrough discoveries. *Strategic Management Journal, 22*(6–7), 521–543.

Arkes, H. R., & Ayton, P. (1999). The sunk cost and Concorde effects: Are humans less rational than lower animals? *Psychological Bulletin, 125*(5), 591–600.

Arkes, H. R., & Blumer, C. (1985). The psychology of sunk cost. *Organizational Behavior and Human Decision Processes, 35*(1), 124–140.

Austin, R. D., Devin, L., & Sullivan, E. E. (2012). Accidental innovation: Supporting valuable unpredictability in the creative process. *Organization Science, 23*(5), 1505–1522.

Barron, G., & Yechiam, E. (2002). Private e-mail requests and the diffusion of responsibility. *Computers in Human Behavior, 18*(5), 507–520.

Bazerman, M. H., Giuliano, T., & Appelman, A. (1984). Escalation of commitment in individual and group decision making. *Organizational Behavior and Human Performance, 33*(2), 141–152.

Beu, D. S., Buckley, M. R., & Harvey, M. G. (2000). The role of pluralistic ignorance in the perception of unethical behavior. *Journal of Business Ethics, 23*(4), 353–364.

Blair, C. A., Thompson, L. F., & Wuensch, K. L. (2005). Electronic helping behavior: The virtual presence of others makes a difference. *Basic and Applied Social Psychology, 27*(2), 171–178.

Bledow, R., Carette, B., Kühnel, J., & Bister, D. (2017). Learning from others' failures: The effectiveness of failure stories for managerial learning. *Academy of Management Learning & Education, 16*(1), 39–53.

Bolstad, I. (2017, 23rd January). *Interviewer: Ø. Kvalnes.*
Bond, J. (2008). The blame culture—An obstacle to improving safety. *Journal of Chemical Health and Safety, 15*(2), 6–9.
Brand, A. (1998). Knowledge management and innovation at 3M. *Journal of Knowledge Management, 2*(1), 17–22.
Buchanan, R. (1992). Wicked problems in design thinking. *Design Issues, 8*(2), 5–21.
Cannon, M. D., & Edmondson, A. C. (2005). Failing to learn and learning to fail (intelligently): How great organizations put failure to work to innovate and improve. *Long Range Planning, 38*(3), 299–319.
Chiu, Y.-P., & Chang, S.-C. (2015). Leverage between the buffering effect and the bystander effect in social networking. *CyberPsychology, Behavior & Social Networking, 18*(8), 450–456.
Collins, J. C. (2001). *Good to great: Why some companies make the leap… and others don't.* New York, NY: Random House.
Cook, P. (2016). *Leading innovation, creativity, and enterprise.* London: Bloomsbury.
Darley, J. M., & Latané, B. (1968). Bystander intervention in emergencies: Diffusion of responsibility. *Journal of Personality and Social Psychology, 8*(4), 377–383.
Edmondson, A. C. (2011). Strategies for learning from failure. *Harvard Business Review, 89,* 48–55.
Fischer, P., Greitemeyer, T., Kastenmüller, A., Krueger, J. I., Vogrincic, C., Frey, D., … Kainbacher, M. (2011). The bystander-effect: A meta-analytic review on bystander intervention in dangerous and non-dangerous emergencies. *Psychological Bulletin, 137*(4), 517–537.
Fischer, P., Greitemeyer, T., Pollozek, F., & Frey, D. (2006). The unresponsive bystander: Are bystanders more responsive in dangerous emergencies? *European Journal of Social Psychology, 36*(2), 267–278.
Friedman, D., Pommerenke, K., Lukose, R., Milam, G., & Huberman, B. A. (2007). Searching for the sunk cost fallacy. *Experimental Economics, 10*(1), 79–104.
Gelb, D. (Writer). (2015). Massimo Bottura. In Netflix (Producer), *Chef's Table.*
Gilad, B., Kaish, S., & Loeb, P. D. (1987). Cognitive dissonance and utility maximization: A general framework. *Journal of Economic Behavior & Organization, 8*(1), 61–73.

Govindarajan, V., & Srinivas, S. (2013). Innovation mindset: We can see it in action at 3M. *Leadership Excellence Essentials, 30*(11), 7–8.

Hart, W., Albarracín, D., Eagly, A. H., Brechan, I., Lindberg, M. J., & Merrill, L. (2009). Feeling validated versus being correct: A meta-analysis of selective exposure to information. *Psychological Bulletin, 135*(1), 555–588.

Hoholm, T. (2011). *The contrary forces of innovation: An ethnography of innovation in the food industry.* London: Springer.

Kahneman, D., & Tversky, A. (1979). Prospect theory: An analysis of decision under risk. *Econometrica, 47*(2), 263–291.

Kolko, J. (2015). Design thinking comes of age. *Harvard Business Review, 93*(9), 66–69.

Kreitz, C., Furley, P., Memmert, D., & Simons, D. J. (2016). The influence of attention set, working memory capacity, and expectations on inattentional blindness. *Perception, 45*(4), 386–399.

Latané, B. (1981). The psychology of social impact. *American Psychologist, 36*(4), 343–356.

Latané, B., & Darley, J. M. (1976). *Help in a crisis: Bystander response to an emergency.* Morristown, NJ: General Learning Press.

Latané, B., & Nida, S. A. (1981). Ten years of research on group size and helping. *Psychological Bulletin, 89*(2), 308–324.

Lee, F., Edmondson, A. C., Thomke, S., & Worline, M. (2004). The mixed effects of inconsistency on experimentation in organizations. *Organization Science, 15*(3), 310–326.

Mack, A. (2003). Inattentional blindness. *Current Directions in Psychological Science, 12*(5), 180–184.

Nickerson, R. S. (1998). Confirmation bias: A ubiquitous phenomenon in many guises. *Review of General Psychology, 2*(2), 175–220.

Parfit, D. (1984). *Reasons and persons.* Oxford: Oxford University Press.

Plötner, M., Over, H., Carpenter, M., & Tomasello, M. (2015). Young children show the bystander effect in helping situations. *Psychological Science, 26*(4), 499–506.

Rami, U., & Gould, C. (2016). From a "culture of blame" to an encouraged "learning from failure culture". *Business Perspectives & Research, 4*(2), 161–168.

Shefrin, H. (2007). *Behavioral corporate finance: Decisions that create value B2—Behavioral corporate finance: Decisions that create value.* New York: McGraw-Hill Irwin.

Shepherd, D. A., Patzelt, H., & Wolfe, M. (2011). Moving forward from project failure: Negative emotions, affective commitment, and learning from experience. *Academy of Management Journal, 54*(6), 1229–1259.

Simons, D. J., & Chabris, C. F. (1999). Gorillas in our midst: Sustained inattentional blindness for dynamic events. *Perception, 28*(9), 1059–1074.

Staw, B. M. (1976). Knee-deep in the big muddy: A study of escalating commitment to a chosen course of action. *Organizational Behavior and Human Performance, 16*(1), 27–44.

Steinhoff, L., & Palmatier, R. (2016). Understanding loyalty program effectiveness: Managing target and bystander effects. *Journal of the Academy of Marketing Science, 44*(1), 88–107.

Stoop, J. A., & Kahan, J. P. (2005). Flying is the safest way to travel: How aviation was a pioneer in independent accident investigation. *European Journal of Transport and Infrastructure Research, 5*(2), 115–128.

Waring, J. J. (2005). Beyond blame: Cultural barriers to medical incident reporting. *Social Science and Medicine, 60*(9), 1927–1935.

Zhu, D. H., & Westphal, J. D. (2011). Misperceiving the beliefs of others: How pluralistic ignorance contributes to the persistence of positive security analyst reactions to the adoption of stock repurchase plans. *Organization Science, 22*(4), 869–886.

Open Access This chapter is licensed under the terms of the Creative Commons Attribution 4.0 International License (http://creativecommons.org/licenses/by/4.0/), which permits use, sharing, adaptation, distribution and reproduction in any medium or format, as long as you give appropriate credit to the original author(s) and the source, provide a link to the Creative Commons license and indicate if changes were made.

The images or other third party material in this chapter are included in the chapter's Creative Commons license, unless indicated otherwise in a credit line to the material. If material is not included in the chapter's Creative Commons license and your intended use is not permitted by statutory regulation or exceeds the permitted use, you will need to obtain permission directly from the copyright holder.

3

Moral Risk in a Nursing Home

"One fine summer day, a local fisher came to the nursing home door with buckets full of fresh fish that he had just caught from his boat. He wanted to give it to us free of charge. We rejoiced, and thought that now we could create a fish barbecue for the residents. They would be so happy to get fresh food straight from the sea on their plates. The air at the nursing home would be filled with the pleasant smell of grilled fish. Then one of us remembered what the law says about food at the nursing home. Everything we serve as food to the residents has to come from a registered supplier, and the fisher was not on the list. This meant that it would be illegal to grill and serve the fresh fish from the sea at the home. Still we felt that it would be the right thing to do, as it would be such a rich and thrilling experience for the residents" (Norlin & Borvik, 2016).

This event took place at Søbakken, a nursing home in the coastal town of Helgeroa in Norway. A change in leadership there in 2011 brought about swift improvement in the work environment and in the living conditions for the residents. Søbakken had a bad reputation in the local community, both as a place to work and as a place to live. That changed rapidly when nurse Kristine Borvik took over as the leader of the nursing home, with nurse Helén Norlin as the assistant leader. The development at Søbakken has come under scrutiny in a research project, based on data from interviews with employees, residents, relatives, and other people from the local community (Carlsen & Kvalnes, 2015). This chapter builds on further interviews with Borvik and Norlin, to unveil details in narratives concerning moral risk and fallibility at Søbakken. Their initiatives are studied through the lens of a distinction between active and passive mistakes, or between doing something you should not have done, and refraining from doing something you should have done. The activities they generated at the nursing home increased the likelihood of committing active mistakes, and reduced the likelihood of committing passive mistakes.

This chapter addresses three principled questions regarding responsibility and risk at work: (1) To what extent do our moral evaluations of past decisions and behavior depend on actual outcomes? The concept of moral luck (Nagel, 1979; Williams, 1981) captures the paradoxical phenomenon that the way things actually turn out affect verdicts of the right or wrongness of what people do, even though we take morality to be a dimension of behavior where it is only reasonable to hold people responsible for what has been within their control. (2) What kind of protection against sanctions should be in place for people who take risky decisions at work? Moral hazard occurs in situations where people choose high-risk options because they feel insulated against taking the burden if things should end badly. A less acknowledged phenomenon is what we may call moral paralysis, where people become passive because they feel that they will have to take the burden alone if things should end badly. Moral hazard can lead to an overload of active mistakes, while moral paralysis can encourage passive mistakes. (3) What is the role of leaders in cases where either active or passive mistakes from employees lead to bad outcomes? The Søbakken activities did not lead to serious harm to residents, but might have done so, and that would have been at the test of the extent to which their closest local council leader would have stood by or distanced herself from the nursing home leaders.

The narratives in this chapter are mainly from a nursing home, but the discussion points to theoretical and practical implications beyond that field of work, with regard to how organizations (1) cope with moral luck, (2) strike a balance between moral hazard and moral paralysis, and to how (3) leaders provide support to exposed and vulnerable employees in critical situations.

1 Active and Passive Mistakes

Crucial to the positive development at Søbakken was an initiative from the new leaders to involve employees and residents in reflections about how they wanted life to be there. The nurses started by asking them a very fundamental set of questions: What do you want? What is a good life for you here? (Carlsen & Kvalnes, 2015) In a reflection note, Borvik and Norlin write: "We have experienced that it is smart to dig some more when we ask our residents, and not be satisfied with "everything is OK, or I don't know …". We ask them what they used to do earlier in life when they were younger. What did you enjoy during the summer, when you were younger? If they cannot answer themselves, we ask a relative" (Norlin & Borvik, 2015).

The answers from the residents exposed misunderstandings about daily routines and preferences, but also a much more fundamental desire. The old people who lived at Søbakken wanted to have more contact with life. Currently, they felt separated from meaningful activity, stored away from the rest of the community, out of sight, to wither and die. Many of the projects and initiatives at Søbakken in the months and years to follow attempted to bring the residents closer to the life outside the walls of the nursing home, both by inviting people outsiders of all ages in, and by taking the residents on trips. Activities like sightseeing bus tours, beer brewing, mini-concerts, exercise sessions, bazaars, boat trips, public reading sessions, Christmas tree lighting, visits from the local school band, and bathing trips to the sea, contributed to bringing the residents closer to life. The residents came more in touch with the community in which they had grown up and lived earlier (Carlsen & Kvalnes, 2015).

Autonomy and social functioning are important to human well-being at all stages of life, including old age (Bangerter, Heid, Abbott, & Van Haitsma, 2016; Paque, Goossens, Elseviers, Van Bogaert, & Dilles, 2016).

Bringing an old person out of his or her isolation at a nursing home and in tighter contact with life is in itself a commendable initiative, but will sometimes involve a raised risk of personal harm to that person. Moral risk is the kind of risk that exposes the decision-maker to moral criticism and blame, based on whether things go well or not. If the outcome is fine, the instigators are likely to receive praise, while if something goes wrong and the old person is harmed in some way, they can become subject to criticism and blame, and more formally to legal repercussions. One basic challenge for the leaders at Søbakken was that in order to meet the residents' desire to come closer to life again, they also on some occasions had to increase the risk of harm, and thus expose themselves to moral risk. Going on a bus trip to the sea with fragile, old people involves more risk that something will go wrong than keeping them in the sofa back at the nursing home. One fragile old woman expressed an eager desire to swim in the sea, an activity she had loved earlier in life, but there was no way of telling in advance how her body would respond when it was brought into the rather cold sea water. The trip from the nursing home to the sea was also one where small accidents could affect her badly. Movement and activity are good in itself, but will be seen in a different light by relatives, authorities, and the media if someone ends up with a heart failure, a concussion or a broken hip bone. The woman did get her desire fulfilled, and had a wonderful experience in the water, but taking her there was a risky endeavor.

We can apply a distinction between active and passive mistakes in order to conceptualize the change in moral orientation at Søbakken. You make an active mistake if you do something that you should not have done, and a passive mistake if you refrain from doing something that you should have done. In many work settings, the balance and priority between active or passive mistakes can make a considerable difference to practice. In surgery, the doctors can face situations of doubt about whether a patient suffers from appendicitis or not, and must decide to operate or not. Operating on a person who does not in fact have appendicitis will constitute an active mistake, doing something one should not have done, while sending a person with appendicitis home without surgery will be a passive mistake, refraining from doing something one should actually have done. During a year, the team of doctors may face a number of doubt cases, and they are likely to make mistakes. They can make a conscious choice about what kind of mistake they are prepared to tolerate the most, either operating on someone who in fact does not need it, thus creating unnecessary complications and exposure to harm to that person, or failing to operate on someone who actually needs it, and prolonging the suffering for that person.

In a finance setting, the difference between active and passive mistakes can occur with regard to evaluations of which customers should and should not get a particular kind of loan. Even here, we can imagine a set of doubtful cases, where it is uncertain whether customers are capable of handling the loan for which they have applied. It can be an active mistake to provide a loan to someone who will not be able to repay it and will have his or her economy put in jeopardy because of it. It will be a passive mistake to refuse a loan to someone who would be able to handle it well, and may now not be able to pursue a particular project, due to a lack of funding. Even in the bank context, a decision can be made regarding a higher or lower tolerance for active and passive mistakes.

In a nursing home, an active mistake can be to initiate some specific activity that leads to harm to one or more residents, while a passive mistake can be to refrain from doing something that would have been good and beneficial for them. The development at Søbakken involved a move towards taking risks that might end up as active mistakes, since they might have harmful outcomes. The established routines that the residents complained about, being stored away and separated from life, seemed designed to avoid active mistakes, with the unacknowledged consequence of making passive mistakes of not giving them sufficient exercise and movement, and distancing them from the local community.

The practice of pacifying residents in a nursing home can be seen as a result of omission bias, or the assumption that harmful outcomes of actions (active mistakes) are more serious and important to avoid than harmful outcomes of omissions (passive mistakes) (Asch et al., 1994; Baron & Ritov, 2004; Ritov & Baron, 1990; Spranca, Minsk, & Baron, 1991). Omission bias indicates a more or less conscious preference for harm caused by omissions over equal or lesser harm caused by acts. Omission bias can affect vaccination decisions, in that many people consider the risk of harm from vaccination as more serious than the risk from omitting vaccination (Ritov & Baron, 1990). There is a link here to attitudes towards risky play, discussed in chapter one. Harms that might occur when children climb trees or roam their neighborhood can be considered as more serious than the less tangible harms caused by shutting them off from those activities. Childhood research tells us that passivity in children can have a bad impact on their mental and physical development, but for a concerned and anxious parent, that consequence can appear to be more acceptable than the harm that can result from risky play (Sandseter & Kennair, 2011). Applied to a nursing home environment, omission bias can mean that harm caused by initiatives to activate residents are seen as more serious than harms from leaving residents with limited scope of action in their beds or rooms.

Omission bias can be placed in the context of a tendency to formulate ethics in proscriptive terms (this is what we should not do), with an emphasis on avoiding harm, and not in prescriptive terms (this is what we should do), where the aim is to advance positive outcomes (Carnes & Janoff-Bulman, 2012). This line of thinking builds on Kant's distinction between negative and positive moral duty, between the moral duty to do no harm, and the moral duty to do good for others. A proscriptive ethics has low tolerance for active mistakes and a higher tolerance for passive mistakes, and vice versa for a prescriptive ethics, The activities at Søbakken that came as responses to the residents' wish to come closer to life indicate a prescriptive ethics, since the main motivation was to make positive differences in the lives of elderly people. Initiatives did raise the probability that active mistakes would occur, but lowered the probability of passive mistakes. The previous regime at the nursing home seems to have advocated a proscriptive ethics, with emphasis on safety and avoiding injury, and that appears to be the norm in the nursing of elderly people in Norway.

The commitment to bring residents closer to life, even at the expense of increased risk of harm, raises principled questions about the tolerance for active and passive mistakes. The next section returns to the opening narrative of whether to arrange a fish barbecue for the residents at Søbakken. The concept of moral luck can be useful in shedding light on the issues that are at stake in that situation, since it emphasizes how actual outcomes color the moral judgements we tend to make.

2   The Fish Dilemma

The local fisher had noticed the positive development at Søbakken, and wanted to contribute in his own way. That is why he turned up one morning with buckets full of fresh fish. The leaders at the nursing home wanted to make a barbecue for the residents, but realized that the law forbids them to do so. Fish should come frozen or vacuum packed from a registered supplier that would guarantee its quality and safety. That legal requirement makes sense from the perspective of food safety and protecting the residents from harm. Fish can be contaminated or contain hazardous bones, and so pose a threat to the health of those who eat it. From a proscriptive standpoint, then, one should not serve fish from a local fisher, no matter how tempting that might be. On the other hand, from a prescriptive standpoint, one should try to enrich people's lives when there is an opportunity to do so. A barbecue with fresh fish would be a thrilling and memorable event for the residents at Søbakken, one they would know to appreciate in full.

A decision to break the law and serve the fresh fish could be seen as an instance of civil disobedience, a situation where otherwise law-abiding citizens give priority to moral considerations over legal ones, because they think the law is unreasonable. A justification of this kind can be interpreted to belong at the sixth stage of moral development, identified in Kohlberg's theory of moral development (Kohlberg, 1973). On this stage, decisions are based on the application of universal ethical principles that are considered to be above local law and legislation. It is a stage where the Golden Rule and related principles like Kant's categorical imperative dominate. Interviews with the leaders at Søbakken indicate that the principled question they asked themselves in times of doubt was whether they would have accepted that their own parents were subject to the decisions under consideration. Putting yourself in the shoes of those affected by your own decision is a typical ingredient of principled moral reasoning. In the fish dilemma, the leaders at

Søbakken reasoned about whether they would have accepted that the nursing home where their own parents stayed, arranged a grill party where they illegally served fresh fish from an unregistered supplier.

The fact that someone's moral reasoning follows the pattern described by Kohlberg as belonging to the highest and most mature form of moral development is no indication that the decision is correct. Lunatics can reason in ways that perfectly follow the procedure drawn up in the maxims of Kant's categorical imperative. We can distinguish between the form and content of moral reasoning, and suffice to say here is that considering to set the law aside and prioritizing one's own moral convictions has the form of Kohlberg's sixth stage moral reasoning.

Opposition to the principled line of thinking at Kohlberg's highest stage could come from someone on the fifth stage, where the emphasis is placed on social contracts and decisions based on democratic and professional procedures (Kohlberg, 1973). The topic was raised in the interview with the pilot Jarle Gimmestad. His general stance is to assume that one should do things by the book, since the rules and procedures have been designed under more or less ideal conditions, by people who are competent and well informed. "When you are in a heated situation, with limited access to information and pressure to make a quick decision, you can assume that the outlined rules have been established by calm heads, who have had time to consider the ramifications of the various alternatives" (Gimmestad, 2016). Kohlberg ranks the social contract reasoning below that of the principled, universal one, but that in itself does not suffice to say that a decision based on the latter is better than one based on the former.

True to their prescriptive stance, the leaders at Søbakken decided to create a barbecue for the residents. In an email, Helén Norlin explained: "One of our aims at the nursing home was to create "the good life" for the residents, and we could put many of our ideas and projects under that motto. "The good life" also has to do with trusting people in the local community and their wish to contribute to the wellbeing of those living at Søbakken. That included the fisher. We had complete trust in him when he said that the fish was fresh from the sea and of the best quality. Many at the nursing home were personally acquainted with him, and knew that he had the best intentions and was reliable" (Norlin, 2016).

The leaders called in extra volunteers to analyze each piece of fish carefully before it was put on a plate and served to a resident, to minimize the risk of harm. The barbecue was a great success, causing jubilation among the residents. The air was filled with the smells of a good life by the sea, and nobody got hurt in any way. The leaders avoided repercussions for breaking the law and taking the risk.

The author has presented the grill party dilemma to professionals and managers in healthcare and in HSE functions on a number of occasions, and asked them to take a stand. It has been interesting to observe how the case evokes different moral intuitions about whether it is acceptable to go ahead and serve the fish, or not. A majority tends to say yes to the grill party, while a vocal minority says they would turn down that offer, based on a respect for legislation, and in the name of food safety. One leader from a local council, when presented with the case, said he would have taken immediate steps to dismiss the leaders at Søbakken, had the incident happened in his organization. He did not accept the fact that the grill party created happiness and joy among the residents and employees as evidence that it was morally right and acceptable to initiate it. Instead, he was concerned about the lack of respect for legislation, and what could follow of further unlawful actions, once this one was deemed acceptable.

It is likely that the responses to the grill party would have been dramatically different if one or more of the residents had actually got a fishbone stuck in the throat or been harmed in some other way. People may applaud risk-taking when things go well, but if they go through some unfortunate circumstance they do not and somebody is injured, the judgement may be less positive, and even critical. The concept of moral luck highlights how actual outcomes affect moral evaluations of what people do and fail to do (Nagel, 1979; Williams, 1981). It was been widely discussed from a range of philosophical and practical perspectives (Biss, 2016; Hankins, 2016; Levy, 2016; Statman, 2015; Whittington, 2015). Moral luck appears to be an oxymoron, in that we are prone to think that the moral quality of what we do cannot depend on circumstances beyond our control. In reality, actual outcomes do affect our moral judgements, as Nagel notes.

> Whether we succeed or fail in what we try to do nearly always depends to some extent on factors beyond our control. This is true of murder, altruism, revolution, the sacrifice of certain interests over others – almost any morally important act. What has been done, and what is morally judged, is partly determined by external factors. However jewel-like the good will may be in its own right, there is a morally significant difference between rescuing someone from burning building and dropping him from a twelfth-storey window while trying to rescue him. Similarly, there is a morally significant difference between reckless driving and manslaughter. But whether a reckless driver hits a pedestrian depends on the presence of the pedestrian at the point where he recklessly passes the red light. (Nagel, 1979, p. 28)

The jewel-metaphor Nagel alludes to is from Kant's description of the good will, the motivation to act, which the German thinker considered as the only proper object of moral judgement, since it has full value in and of itself, independently of outcomes. In opposition to that view, Nagel draws attention to how external factors affect even the description of the act itself, of what a person has done. There is a morally significant difference, he argues, between a successful and an unsuccessful rescue attempt.

Similarly, we can say that there is a morally significant difference between creating a barbecue and a rich sensory experience of a good life for an elderly person, and giving him or her a final and painful meal. Theoretically, we may be convinced by Kant's argument regarding the good will, but once that moral reasoning exercise is over, fall back to a habit of giving moral weight to actual outcomes. There is a considerable tension between the general conviction that morality is unaffected by luck, and the particular moral judgements that are significantly influenced by how things happen to turn out. If a resident gets a bone in the throat and dies during the barbecue, it will affect the moral judgement of the decision to break the law and serve the fish.

Food was also at the core of smaller, everyday dilemmas at Søbakken, where the motivation to improve the quality of life for the residents came up against legal restrictions on what they could eat. One recurring issue was that residents would sometimes not be ready to eat at the specified times for serving hot food, because they were tired or asleep or indisposed in other ways. The solution could then be to reheat the food 2 or 3 hours later, when they were awake and hungry. However, the option to reheat food was illegal. From a legal point of view, that food should either be eaten in its current state of being cold, or thrown away. The restriction against reheating food is based on food safety and a concern for the health of the residents, and in many or most instances, it appears to be reasonable and make sense. At Søbakken, they decided to take a principled approach to each separate situation, and sometimes ended up making the evaluation that this particular instance of reheating food would not pose a health threat, and was morally acceptable. Sometimes they would put leftover potatoes in the fridge overnight, and fry and serve them the next day, instead of throwing what they saw as perfectly fine food (Norlin & Borvik, 2016). Again, the responses to these small instances of civil disobedience and priority to personal, principled moral reasoning over Norwegian legislation, would have been seen in a completely different light if it had happened to cause harm to one or more residents.

3 Moral Hazard and Moral Paralysis

Attitudes towards moral luck from the decision-maker's perspective are likely to depend on the perception of personal cost. To what extent will I have to bear a personal burden if things go badly? In the moral risk literature, emphasis tends to be on the phenomenon of moral hazard, or on how people who feel protected against negative costs of their actions, tend to take higher risk than they otherwise would have done, due to the perception that they will not have to bear the burden if things go wrong. Moral hazard occurs when an insurance customer takes a higher risk with his or her properties, based on the knowledge that if things go wrong, the insurance company will pay the cost (Aron-Dine, Einav, Finkelstein, & Cullen, 2015; Parsons, 2003; Sealey, Gandar, & Mazumdar, 2016). In the classical sense, moral hazard in insurance refers to "(t)he possibility that the policyholder, knowing that he is insured, will change his behavior in a way that produces undesirable outcomes: in particular, he may become more careless" (Parsons, 2003, p. 448). More generally, a person insulated from risk, may become careless and engage in more risk taking than he would have done if he had been fully exposed to risk. He or she is less careful, since the cost of any mishaps for the most part will be taken care of by other parties. Most insurance companies are keenly aware of the dangers of moral hazard, and are therefore wary of offering conditions where the customers only have to take an insignificant part of the burden in case of an accident.

Moral hazard also occurs when banks and other financial institutions engage in reckless transactions and investments, on the assumption that the authorities will save them if the market collapses. In work settings, the highest ranked professionals in an organization can engage in harassment and other anti-social behavior, expecting that their expertise and status as being irreplaceable experts will protect them against sanctions. Under such conditions, the agents do not fear moral luck, because they perceive themselves as invulnerable. For this reason, they may not hesitate to engage in an activity that may turn out to go horribly wrong. More specifically, moral hazard occurs in health care settings where the moral risks in relation to different treatments are measured (Antommaria & King, 2016; Brunnquell & Michaelson, 2016).

The distinction between active and passive mistakes is useful in identifying the behavioral consequences of moral hazard. Human beings make mistakes of both kinds, but under a moral hazard regime, it is more likely that active mistakes dominate. The decision-maker worries less about the personal consequences, and takes more risk than if he or she would have had to take the burden of failure. From the decision-maker's perspective, moral hazard neutralizes the threat of bad moral luck: It may exist, but that is not a worry for a person who experiences protection against punishment or other forms of negative consequences for having caused bad outcomes.

Another important and somehow neglected phenomenon in decision-making and moral risk is on the other side of the perceived protection spectrum from moral hazard. A decision-maker who feels fully exposed to repercussion in the event of a bad outcome, even when the risk he or she have taken appears to have been reasonable, will tend to act in an overtly cautious manner, and avoid doing anything that might conceivably end up badly. Fear of bad moral luck can lead to what we may call moral paralysis, a passive and cautious pattern of conduct. The decision-maker expects blame and criticism, even if the unfortunate unfolding of events has been highly unexpected, and strongly influenced by unforeseeable circumstances. If things go wrong, they expect to be alone in having to take the moral burden, with limited or no support from the organization or network to which they belong. With moral paralysis, a decision-maker will tend to avoid what could turn out to be active mistakes, and thus end up making passive mistakes instead.

In school settings, moral paralysis can lead teachers to keep children indoors to avoid responsibility for harmful consequences of risky play in the schoolyard. A report from the Association of Teachers and Lecturers in the United Kingdom documents widespread bans on traditional children's games in schools, and prohibitions against letting pupils play outside in the snow in winter, out of fear that they might slip and hurt themselves (ATL, 2011). The report connects a sharp decline in field trips outside the schools to the demand for detailed risk assessments of the situations that might occur during such trips. It has created a reluctance amongst teachers to take personal responsibility for harm to the pupils, no matter how unexpected and improbable. As noted in chapter one, risky play in childhood can have a crucial anti-phobic effect, in that it allows children to gain experiences in dealing with dangerous situations (Sandseter & Kennair, 2011). Moral paralysis amongst preschool and school teachers, then, can have the negative effect of barring children from engaging in healthy anti-phobic activities. Avoiding the active mistake of allowing children be involved in play that actually harms them, takes precedence over avoiding the passive mistake of isolating children from potentially important learning experiences.

Moral luck is a worry for a decision-maker operating under moral paralysis, because he or she will personally have to bear the burden of actual negative outcomes. It calls for cautious decision-making and behavior, a risk-averse attitude geared towards not being involved in any kind of activity that might conceivably harm anyone, the moral equivalent of strict liability in law.

Moral reasoning and decision-making in organizations need to find a path between the polarities of moral hazard and moral paralysis, a golden mean between excessive and stifled moral risk-taking among professionals.

Applied to a nursing home context, we can imagine that the decision-makers face one hundred situations where they have the opportunity to enrich the lives of the residents by exposing them to risk of harm. Under moral hazard conditions, they do not have personal incentives to be cautious, and can thus end up choosing the risky option every time, while under moral paralysis conditions, they will have to bear the personal burden in case of an accident, and may therefore reject the risky option every time. The middle ground is one where leaders and employees at a nursing home will sometimes take chances and involve the residents in activities that are at once enriching and potentially harmful, and at other times say no to these options.

4   Supportive Leadership

The two leaders at Søbakken started a range of activities with the residents at the nursing home, in order to meet their desire to come closer to life, and some of them involved a raised risk of harm. In taking these decisions and initiatives, they had the support of their own leader in the local council. She was a person they would call in moments of doubt, in order to get clearance for going ahead with a risky plan. The narratives from Søbakken indicate that the decision-making and activities took place in the middle ground between moral hazard and moral paralysis, that is, between the extremes of being fully insulated against negative consequences of one's own actions, and of being alone in bearing the cost of any unwelcome outcome of one's decisions. The resolve of the local council leader to stand by the leaders at Søbakken in case of an accident or misadventure was never put to the test, because such situations never happened. To some extent, that leader may have had good moral luck in the circumstances she faced. Nagel describes this category of moral luck as follows:

> The things we are called upon to do, the moral tests we face, are importantly determined by factors beyond our control. It may be true of someone that in a dangerous situation he would have behaved in a cowardly or heroic fashion, but if the situation never arises, he will never have the

chance to distinguish or disgrace himself in this way, and his moral record will be different. ... (O)ne is morally at the mercy of fate, and it may seem irrational on reflection, but our ordinary moral judgements would be unrecognizable without it. We judge people for what they actually do or fail to do, not just for what they would have done if circumstances had been different. (Nagel, 1979, pp. 33–34)

Along this line of thinking, the council leader who supported the proscriptive activities and initiatives at Søbakken may have lived up to her word of standing by the decision-makers even in the face of an actual misadventure, or not. She never had the chance to distinguish or disgrace herself in this manner, and so may either have had bad or good circumstantial moral luck in that regard.

Other leaders have had their abilities to stand by their subordinates tested and exposed. In 2007, two ambulance workers in Oslo experienced a lack of leadership support in the aftermath of an incident where they mistakenly thought a person did not need to be taken to the hospital (Schjenken, 2008; Østli, 2008, 2009). During a dramatic encounter in a crowded park in Oslo, one person had been knocked down, and was bleeding from a head wound. The ambulance personnel checked him to find out if he would need further treatment at the hospital. They thought that he probably was on drugs, and decided to get him to his feet and take him to the hospital. Once on his feet, the man started to pee on the shoes and trousers of one of the ambulance people, and then went over to the ambulance and peed on that as well. Now the two professionals reconsidered their initial judgement, and thought the wounded man should be handed over to the police, who were also present. Surrounded by an angry crowd, the ambulance personnel decided to leave the park without the injured man. Later, it turned out that the wounded man had serious head injuries, and these most likely caused his aggressive behavior. He should have been taken immediately to hospital for treatment, and the delay in treatment probably worsened his condition (Østli, 2008).

The wounded man was dark skinned, and on the day after the incident, Kristin Halvorsen, the Finance Minister of Norway indicated that the ambulance personnel was racists. "Could this have happened to a white father of small children? Probably not." (Magnus, 2007) The two ambulance workers received heavy criticism for racism, negligence, and bad professional work. In the beginning, the hospital leadership appeared to stand by them, but as the media storm increased in intensity, they decided to suspend the two, and start internal investigations. The top leaders at the hospital expressed concern for the reputation of the organization, and saw it fit to distance themselves from the two employees. The two ambulance workers were forbidden by their employer to make statements in the media about the incident, while the critical voices could be heard everywhere (Østli, 2008).

During the suspension, one of the ambulance workers quit his job, while the other decided to go public with his version of the story. He was a vastly experienced ambulance driver, with more than 100.000 previous assignments during 17 years, without negative remarks. Before the dramatic event in the park, he had just washed the ambulance clean of blood and urine from a previous incident, and he and his colleague had further assignments on the same day, after the park incident (Schjenken, 2008). Little did they know that their professional lives would be ruined because of a serious mistake in the park. The second ambulance worker also initially quit his job at the hospital, and later won a High Court case against one of the newspapers that labeled him a racist (Johansen, 2014).

Apparently, the ambulance personnel did not receive proper leadership support in the aftermath of the incident (Østli, 2008, 2009). They made a serious passive mistake, in not taking the injured man to the hospital, and had to take the total burden of the negative outcome on their own shoulders. The driver who has been most public about his experiences has talked openly about mental problems and thoughts of suicide. The top leadership at the hospital made it clear that they did not want to see him back in activities where he would have direct contact with patients, the kind of work he had excelled in previously (Østli, 2008). They questioned his ability to do the kind of work he found the most meaningful, helping and making a positive difference to other people. The hospital did have a psychological service for employees, but did not actively offer it in this case. It is very likely that the personal outcomes for the employees would have been vastly different if the leaders had stood up for them and offered support in the aftermath of the dramatic park incident (Østli, 2008).

Social workers are another group of professionals who face constant risks to their moral integrity, in that they have to make decisions that can negatively affect the lives of others. They, too, are vulnerable to bad moral luck (Hollis & Howe, 1987). A child may be at possible risk from parents, and the social workers must decide whether to remove the child from its home. The distinction between active and passive mistakes is relevant here. During one year, the social workers may remove children that would actually have been remained unharmed by parents, an active mistake, and also decide not to remove children, who as it happens turns out to be harmed by parents, a passive mistake. The former kind of mistake cannot easily be documented, in the way the latter can. Ambulance workers encounter a similar challenge in balancing between intervention and help, and deciding that the persons in pain will manage well without professional assistance. Mistakes will occur in these circumstances. They are moral minefields, and the professionals who work under this kind of pressure to their morality deserve leadership support, even at the risk of weakened reputation. A leader, who prioritizes short-term reputational gain over long-term support for employees under pressure, is likely to lose internal credibility in the organization.

This chapter has explored the concept of moral risk, and the distinction between active and passive mistakes, primarily by using examples from the nursing home context of Søbakken. It has focused on three questions that have both theoretical and practical aspects: (1) To what extent do our moral evaluations of past decisions and behavior depend on actual outcomes? The concept of moral luck captures a paradoxical dimension of moral reasoning. On the one hand, we tend to assume that people should only be held responsible for aspects of their decision-making and conduct that are within their control. On the other hand, it seems to make a morally relevant difference whether we succeed or fail in our endeavors to help or support other people. We have seen that omission bias is the tendency to judge harm caused by action to be more serious than the similar harm that comes about through omission or inaction. The Søbakken activities enriched the residents' lives in multiple ways, but also in some cases increased the likelihood of harm. The leaders at the nursing home generated a shift from a proscriptive ethics, accentuating the negative duty of not hurting others, to a prescriptive ethics, answering to the positive duty of creating wellbeing and a good life. That move made it relevant to pose the question of (2) what kind of protection against sanctions should be in place for people who take risky decisions at work. The suggestion in this chapter has been that there is a need to find a middle ground between moral hazard, where people feel insulated against taking the burden if things should end badly, and moral paralysis, where people become passive because they feel that they will have to take the burden alone if things should end badly. Moral hazard can lead to an overload of active mistakes, while moral paralysis can encourage passive mistakes. Leaders are the prime initiators of practices to handle moral risk. Thus, the latter part of the chapter has addressed (3) what the role of leaders is in cases where either active or passive mistakes from employees lead to bad outcomes. These are the situations where the leaders' ability to stand by their subordinates comes to the test, and where some fail, while others truly excel.

References

Antommaria, A. H. M., & King, R. (2016). Moral hazard and transparency in pediatrics: A different problem requiring a different solution.

Aron-Dine, A., Einav, L., Finkelstein, A., & Cullen, M. (2015). Moral hazard in health insurance: Do dynamic incentives matter? *Review of Economics and Statistics, 97*(4), 725–741.

Asch, D. A., Baron, J., Hershey, J. C., Kunreuther, H., Meszaros, J., Ritov, I., et al. (1994). Omission bias and pertussis vaccination. *Medical Decision Making, 14*(2), 118–123.

ATL. (2011). *The Association of Teachers and Lecturers: Over-zelous schools ban British bulldag and conkers*. Retrieved from https://www.atl.org.uk/Images/18%20April%202011%20-%20Over-zealous%20schools%20ban%20British%20bulldog%20and%20conkers%20-%20ATL.pdf.

Bangerter, L. R., Heid, A. R., Abbott, K., & Van Haitsma, K. (2016). Honoring the everyday preferences of nursing home residents: Perceived choice and satisfaction with care. *The Gerontologist*, gnv697.

Baron, J., & Ritov, I. (2004). Omission bias, individual differences, and normality. *Organizational Behavior and Human Decision Processes, 94*(2), 74–85.
Biss, M. (2016). Radical moral imagination and moral luck. *Metaphilosophy, 47*(4–5), 558–570.
Brunnquell, D., & Michaelson, C. M. (2016). Moral hazard in pediatrics. *The American Journal of Bioethics, 16*(7), 29–38.
Carlsen, A., & Kvalnes, Ø. (2015). *Lightness of radical change: On the positive transformation of a nursing home*. Paper presented at the Academy of Management, Vancouver.
Carnes, N., & Janoff-Bulman, R. (2012). Harm, help, and the nature of (im) moral (in) action. *Psychological Inquiry, 23*(2), 137–142.
Gimmestad, J. (2016, 18th November). Interviewer: Ø. Kvalnes.
Hankins, K. (2016). Adam Smith's intriguing solution to the problem of moral luck. *Ethics, 126*(3), 711–746.
Hollis, M., & Howe, D. (1987). Moral risks in social work. *Journal of Applied Philosophy, 4*(2), 123–133.
Johansen, G. S. (2014). Erik Schjenken vant i Høyesterett. *Journalisten.*
Kohlberg, L. (1973). *Collected papers on moral development and moral education*. Harvard University, Center for Moral Education.
Levy, N. (2016). Dissolving the puzzle of resultant moral luck. *Review of Philosophy and Psychology, 7*(1), 127–139.
Magnus, G. (2007, 10th August). Ville neppe hendt hvit småbarnsfar. *Aftenposten.*
Nagel, T. (1979). *Moral luck mortal questions*. Cambridge: Cambridge University Press.
Norlin, H. (2016, 10th August). Interviewer: Ø. Kvalnes. e-mail correspondence.
Norlin, H., & Borvik, K. (2015, 15th August). [Reflection note].
Norlin, H., & Borvik, K. (2016, 28th November). Interviewer: Ø. Kvalnes.
Paque, K., Goossens, K., Elseviers, M., Van Bogaert, P., & Dilles, T. (2016). Autonomy and social functioning of recently admitted nursing home residents. *Aging & Mental Health*, 1–7.
Parsons, C. (2003). Moral hazard in liability insurance. *The Geneva Papers on Risk and Insurance Issues and Practice, 28*(3), 448–471.
Ritov, I., & Baron, J. (1990). Reluctance to vaccinate: Omission bias and ambiguity. *Journal of Behavioral Decision Making, 3*(4), 263–277.
Sandseter, E. B. H., & Kennair, L. E. O. (2011). Children's risky play from an evolutionary perspective: The anti-phobic effects of thrilling experiences. *Evolutionary Psychology, 9*(2), 257–284.

Schjenken, E. (2008, 8th April). Hva som skjedde i Sofienbergparken. *Aftenposten*.
Sealey, C. W., Gandar, J. M., & Mazumdar, S. C. (2016). Guaranty funds and moral hazard in the insurance industry: A theoretical perspective. *International Trade and International Finance* (pp. 527–545). Springer.
Spranca, M., Minsk, E., & Baron, J. (1991). Omission and commission in judgment and choice. *Journal of Experimental Social Psychology, 27*(1), 76–105.
Statman, D. (2015). Moral luck and the problem of the innocent attacker. *Ratio, 28*(1), 97–111.
Whittington, L. J. (2015). Getting moral luck right. *The philosophy of luck*, (pp. 205–218). John Wiley & Sons, Inc.
Williams, B. (1981). *Moral luck: Philosophical papers 1973-1980*. Cambridge: Cambridge University Press.
Østli, K. S. (2008). En stemplet mann *Aftenposten/A-Magasinet*.
Østli, K. S. (2009). *Ambulansesaken/Ali Farah-saken*. Oslo.

Open Access This chapter is licensed under the terms of the Creative Commons Attribution 4.0 International License (http://creativecommons.org/licenses/by/4.0/), which permits use, sharing, adaptation, distribution and reproduction in any medium or format, as long as you give appropriate credit to the original author(s) and the source, provide a link to the Creative Commons license and indicate if changes were made.

The images or other third party material in this chapter are included in the chapter's Creative Commons license, unless indicated otherwise in a credit line to the material. If material is not included in the chapter's Creative Commons license and your intended use is not permitted by statutory regulation or exceeds the permitted use, you will need to obtain permission directly from the copyright holder.

4

Coping with Fallibility in Aviation

"After takeoff from Kristiansand on our way to Oslo, we experienced a brake pressure leak that caused some shaking in the plane. We tried the standard procedures to neutralize it, with no effect. Then we tested other options, and found that the shaking stopped when we put on the brakes. The co-pilot and I agreed that of course we would release the brakes before landing. Now we had found an unconventional solution to an immediate problem, and would switch back to the normal non-deployment of the brakes when preparing for landing. Usually, when there is something out of the ordinary that we need to remember, we create a reminder, by taping a piece of paper to the window in the cockpit, or something odd like that. This time we did not do that, since we thought it was unnecessary. Checking that the brakes were off would turn up not only once, but twice in the checklist procedures before landing, so to our minds, there was no risk at all that we would forget to release the brakes. The flight continued, and we did the first check. I answered automatically that brakes are off, without actually thinking and taking them off. Then later, for the second time, we did a checklist procedure, and again I answered as I always do, that brakes are off. The result was that we landed with the brakes on, and it was a very rough and unpleasant experience for the passengers and the staff onboard. The tires exploded, and the plane came to a halt across the runway, and not parallel to it, as it should have. Nobody got seriously injured, but it was a shocking experience for everybody, not easy to shake off and forget" (Gimmestad, 2016).

Jarle Gimmestad is an experienced former pilot, who now works as a safety consultant in industry, healthcare, and travel. His own story about landing with the brakes on serves as evidence that pilots, like the rest of us, are prone to make mistakes. He also uses it as an invitation to participants in seminars about safety to open up about their own professional fallacies and mistakes, lowering the threshold to do so. Once the former pilot has admitted a mistake, it is easier for others to do the same. The conversation can begin about human errors and the ways in which to deal with them.

The introduction to this book included another Gimmestad narrative, about the driver of the pushback tractor who made the pilot aware of dripping from the wing, and who persisted with his feedback, even after the pilot had signaled a stop to the conversation. It illustrates the strong emphasis on teamwork in aviation. Even the lowest ranked employee has a responsibility to intervene in a situation where he or she senses that something is wrong. It is also the responsibility of the highest ranked employee to take such interventions seriously.

The main sources of data for the current chapter are extensive interviews with Gimmestad about safety in aviation. We first met in 2009, when I was writing a book in Norwegian about fallibility at work (Kvalnes, 2010), and have remained in contact since then. The relation has gone beyond that of being researcher and informant, in that we have taught seminars and given conference presentations together, combining theoretical and practical, experience-based input about fallibility at work. The interview method has been one where we talk extensively about narratives and cases, I write them down, get feedback from him about the content, and rewrite the text accordingly. The primary theoretical input in this chapter is a barrier model to structure thinking and activity connected to safety (Reason, 1990). It has applicability beyond aviation and safety. Organizations can use it to (a) create awareness, (b) implement analysis and (c) prepare for action in settings where errors can lead to unwelcome outcomes.

1 Inattentional Blindness

Safety in aviation has improved in recent decades because of a shared realization that pilots are fallible beings. There has been a shift in attitude, from seeing pilots as extraordinary, infallible individuals who could be trusted to bring the plane safely to its destination, to understanding air travel as depending on teamwork, where all the individuals involved depend on feedback and support from others. The realization that each individual is fallible and depends upon others to intervene when he or she appears to make a mistake has caused a breakthrough in safety practices (Helmreich & Davies, 2004; Stoop & Kahan, 2005). The development has been noted in healthcare, where the aviation approach has inspired similar practices of coping with fallibility (Kao & Thomas, 2008; Pronovost, et al., 2009; Aviram, Benyamini, Lewenhoff, & Wilf-Miron, 2003). Strategies for learning from mistakes in healthcare is explored further in the next chapter.

Personal narratives about mistakes are a rich source for learning (Bister, Bledow, Carette, & Kühnel, 2017; Gould & Rami, 2016). Jarle Gimmestad shares a range of stories from his own time in the cockpit with his audiences. A story about the aftermath of the brake incident and how it was handled in his organization, generate further learning points. Two aspects stand out, one regarding knowledge, and another regarding perception. First, his bosses were pondering what to do with Gimmestad after the event, and ended up sending him on a three-days course in how brakes function, thus indicating that what he had been lacking on that dramatic day was basic brake knowledge. They reduced the problem to something concrete and tangible that could be fixed by introducing the pilot to new knowledge. From a philosophical perspective, this can be seen as a contemporary version of Socrates' idea that for a person to do the good, it is enough that he knows the good. As an explanation of Gimmestad's mistake, it seems rather weak and unconvincing. It is unlikely that he forgot to put off the brakes because he did not know about the functioning of the brakes, and would have acted differently if that knowledge had been in his possession at the time of the event. Sending Gimmestad on that course appears to originate from a misunderstanding of the causes of his conduct, a simplistic and technical response to a complex set of challenges connected to fallibility and the interaction between human beings and technology.

Second, the words most emphasized by Gimmestad's main boss in the conversation after the event were that he trusted that there would be no repetition of that particular kind of mistake. "I am sure that you will never again land with the brakes on in your pilot career." He has turned out to be right about that, but on hindsight, Gimmestad believes that his boss' words made him exaggerate his attention to the brakes, at the expense of other and equally important aspects of the situation before, during, and after a flight (Gimmestad, 2016).

When a person is encouraged to focus on one particular aspect of a complex situation, it can lead a blindness to other significant aspects, as documented in studies in perception psychology (Mack, 2003; Chabris & Simons, 1999). When you tell a pilot or a professional in other settings that they are not likely to that particular mistake again, it can create a strong motivation to make your words come true. That in itself can trigger aspect blindness since it draws the professional's attention to one particular aspect of the situation, much as in the gorilla experiment (Chabris & Simons, 1999), mentioned in Chap. 2. Gimmestad says that the period after the dramatic landing was one where he was particularly attentive to the brakes, and made himself vulnerable to overlook other important matters in the cockpit. That might have been the time in his career when the safety of flying with him was at its lowest.

Inattentional blindness is a phenomenon that poses a threat to safety, and to the success of other collaborative processes. One by one, individuals have a limited ability to perceive what goes on around them, and depend upon colleagues to intervene when they are blind to significant aspects of what goes on in their work environment. As noted earlier, the experience of being blind to something that is right in front of their eyes comes as a considerable surprise to participants in experimental studies. It can generate a realization that we are dependent to a high degree of input from other people's perspectives in order to get a rich and adequate understanding of what goes on in our work environment. The next section focuses on a model central to systematic efforts in aviation to counter the pervasive threat of inattentional blindness. It is a model that can be adopted in other organizational settings to create awareness and readiness for action in situations where people make mistakes.

2 A Barrier Model

Over the years, reflection on practice has strengthened safety in aviation. A combination of practical and academic contributions have highlighted the need for precise and direct communication, and a development from a heroic and individualistic approach, to a more collective one, where teamwork is essential. Theoretical contributions from Reason (1990) have been central to this development, first through the establishment of a vocabulary to distinguish between different kinds of error, and second through his so-called Swiss Cheese Model for dealing adequately with error (Reason, 1990). Both of these conceptual sources have relevance beyond aviation, as they can be useful in analyses of fallibility and error outside the safety domain.

Reason distinguishes between execution errors and planning errors. With the former, the plan is fine, but the execution faulty, while with the latter things go wrong from the start, since the plan is inadequate for the task ahead. Furthermore, he separates between two kinds of execution errors, and calls them slips and lapses. Slips are actions not carried out as intended or planned, as when a person struggles with digits on a phone when dialing in a frequency. There can be "Freudian slips" when a person intends to say one thing, but inadvertently ends up saying something revealing about his or her real attitudes or thoughts. The idea is good, but not the execution. Lapses are missed actions and omissions, as when somebody has failed to do something due to lapses of memory or attention, or because they have forgotten something. Gimmestad's landing with the brakes on is an example of a lapse (Reason, 1990).

A student presented another example of a lapse to me at a seminar at the Norwegian Police University College. The agent was a police officer who was an expert at rapidly disarming people who point a gun at him. He had built up this expertise through thousands of repetitions in training. The police officer had asked colleagues and friends countless times to point a gun at him, and he wrestled it off them with amazing speed, repeatedly. When he encountered a real and dangerous situation, coming face to face with a gunman in a supermarket, things went well in the beginning. He used his impressive skill to quickly take the weapon out of the hands of the gunman, thus removing his ability to cause serious harm. Then, the policeman proceeded to hand the weapon back to the gunman, reinstating him in a position to cause harm. That was the movement automated though all the repetitions with colleagues and friends. He had grabbed the weapon, handed it back, grabbed the weapon, handed it back again, repeatedly. The police officer was saved through the intervention of a colleague, who was able to disarm the perplexed gunman a second time. A lesson from this example is that it matters how you frame the training situation, since every movement can become automated, even unwelcome ones like handing a weapon back to the person who initially has it in his or her hands.

Slips and lapses, then, are execution errors. In Reason's vocabulary, they differ from mistakes, which are a type of error brought about by a faulty plan or intention. You make a planning error or mistake when you do something believing that it is the appropriate and correct thing to do, when in fact it is not. As discussed in the previous chapter, we can distinguish between active and passive mistakes, where an active mistake is to do something you should in fact not have done, while a passive mistake is to refrain from doing something you should in fact have done.

A common feature of slips, lapses, and mistakes is that they can start a chain of events that lead to some sort of accident or unfortunate outcome. Reason argues that systematic analyses of accidents need to take into account why the error has occurred. It is easy to start the blame game and point the finger at the person who has slipped, lapsed, or made a mistake, but a thorough understanding of the event at hand needs to clarify the systemic aspects. To what extent have the persons who erred received proper support, training, and guidance? To what extent can long working hours or other potentially stressful factors have contributed to the error? Questions like these are geared towards detecting the root causes of the event, and to keep at bay the understandable instinct to find a scapegoat.

Reason's (1990) Swiss Cheese Model contains three main elements: Error, barriers, and accidents. The main idea is that an error sets in motion a chain of events that leads to an accident, unless there are barriers in place to stop it. Gimmestad started landing procedures with the brakes on, and although that lapse did not result in casualties, the resulting landing constitutes an accident. It could have been avoided if there had been barriers in place to stop the causal chain. Reason distinguishes between three kinds of barrier elements: Technology, procedures and rules, and human intervention. At the time when Gimmestad made the landing with brakes on, there was no technology in place to prevent it from happening. There were procedures to make him and the co-pilot consider the brake issue, but that did not suffice to stop the chain of events either. Finally, the human element could have consisted in an intervention from the co-pilot, who could have challenged Gimmestad and been more alert to the brake issue. Today, technological improvement is in place, making it impossible to replicate the mistake of landing with the brakes on. That came about as an acknowledgement that these are the kinds of errors humans are likely to make, and that cannot be eliminated through training or exercises in awareness.

When a pilot makes a mistake, and the barriers are not sufficiently strong to halt the fatal causal chain it sets in motion, the bad outcome normally occurs quite rapidly, in a matter of seconds or minutes. In other settings, the time from the mistake to the unwanted result can be much longer. On September 8, 1989, Partnair Flight 394 crashed off the coast of Hirtshals in Denmark, and all the fifty five people on board died. The main cause of the crash was a mistake made three years earlier, when cheap, counterfeit aircraft parts where used instead of original ones, to fix the tail of the aircraft. These parts where not of the required quality, and gradually wore out, leading to a collapse of the tail. The mistake of using low-quality parts set in motion a causal chain of events that ended in the fatal accident three years later (*Report on the Convair 340 aircraft accident*, 1993). Inspections of the aircraft could have functioned as barrier elements to stop it, but in this case, there were neither technological, procedural, nor human factors in place to avoid the crash from happening.

I have applied Reason's model in offshore engineering settings, and asked experienced professionals to provide examples from their own work environment, where a mistake can lead to an accident or unwanted event. One engineer said that if he made a mistake on the drawing board today, and nobody, including himself noticed, it could set off a chain of events leading to a bad outcome in about three years, at the bottom of the ocean, where some components in a complex structure would not fit together or not function properly. Even in that kind of work environment, there is a need for efficient barriers to stop the mistake from causing a negative outcome. Technology, procedures, or human intervention can serve to identify the mistake and break off the series of events that otherwise will lead to an unwelcome result. Three years provides more time for a barrier to work, but it might be that the crucial time to detect the mistake and stop it from causing trouble is quite short. If nobody notices anything or takes action in the beginning, there may be no further quality checks of the drawings. The production phase sets in with an undetected mistake on board.

In the engineering context, I inquired about whether people who detect mistakes and intervene receive applause in their work environment. One way to strengthen the barrier system can be to celebrate the instances where a person voices a concern and steps out of passivity. Depending on the size and importance of the project and the savings brought about through the intervention, the active person can receive minor or major hero treatment. The response from the engineering group was that the heroes in their work environment are not those who speak up in critical quality moments, but rather those who step in once an unwelcome event has occurred, at the bottom of the ocean or elsewhere. These are the people who do damage limitation, and are experts at fixing things that are already broken. Things look bleak, but then these exceptional professionals turn up to minimize the negativity. Reflections on this issue brought about a shared realization that even the people who speak up earlier, to stop the unwelcome events to happen in the first place, deserve positive attention in the organization.

The distinction between active and passive mistakes can also help explain reluctance to take an initiative and voice a concern. When you speak up, chances are that you are raising a false alarm, and that constitutes an active mistake, doing something that it turns out you should not have done. To keep quiet in such situations might turn out to be wrong but only constitutes a passive mistake, to refrain from doing something you should have done. You may get away with it more easily than an active mistake. In organizations with a more or less acknowledged preference for passive mistakes over active mistakes, chances are that people opt to say nothing. Efforts to make it normal and appreciated to voice a concern need to build a tolerance for active mistakes in what people perceive to be critical quality moments.

Reason came up with the name Swiss Cheese Model to draw attention to a potential weakness in the barrier mentality he proposed. When people start to think about safety and prevention in barrier terms, they may end up judging the strength of the barrier system in terms of the number of layers it consists in. The more layers, the better. If you have a procedure consisting of safety checks at three different times, it appears to create better safety than if you only have one safety check in place. This way of thinking can create a false sense of safety, according to Reason. He proposes that we should compare each layer in the barrier with a slice of Swiss cheese. What they have in common is a propensity to have large and small holes in them. If we are unlucky, the holes in the barriers are placed next to each other in a way that allows the negative chain of events to travel straight through. We may be content with the high number of layers, but an experience that a negative outcome occurs after all, because we have underestimated the size and positioning of the holes in each layer.

One of my students in a leadership and safety class gave the following example of how a higher number of barrier layers can cause less rather than more safety. She worked in a hospital unit where they sometimes treated dangerous patients, who needed to be checked for weapons and other dangerous objects when they entered and left the premises. It had been the responsibility of the police to check the patients when they went in or out of the hospital. In order to make sure that they came and left unarmed, a second round of checking, conducted by hospital staff, was introduced. The intention was to make the system twice as safe, but in reality, the new system led to lenient controls both by the police and by hospital staff, since both groups had in mind that another group would also check the patient for dangerous objects. The introduction of the second barrier level created a bigger hole in the existing one, and it also came with a hole itself.

The barrier model can also be useful in analyzing creative processes. As discussed in Chap. 2, effective development of new products and services depend on producing intelligent failures as quickly as possible. To persist with a proposal that really is not that good, is a mistake that will lead to a big or small disaster later, unless there are barrier elements in place that cut off the causal chain of events. It takes courage to speak out against a proposal and claim that it should be scrapped.

We can redescribe in barrier terms the three psychological phenomena mentioned as obstacles to detecting and speaking out about mistakes. (1) Sunk cost fallacy can create a weakness in the barrier, if the people who are supposed to intervene and take action when they spot an error, have invested heavily in the development of the idea from which the error generates. In order to intervene and stop the chain of events, they have to admit flaws in their own previous thinking and priorities. That makes them unreliable as contributors to the barrier system. Furthermore, awareness of (2) the bystander effect can counter an unwarranted trust in the barrier system based on numbers. We may think that we can strengthen the human dimension of the barrier system, and the likelihood that someone will intervene in critical situations, by increasing the number of people who are in a position to follow the processes and speak their minds. Research on the bystander effect indicate otherwise. The more people who are included as witnesses to the processes and invited to intervene, the less likely it is that one or some of them will actually do so, due to diffusion of responsibility and doubts about one's own personal judgement. Finally, (3) according to research on the confirmation trap, we tend to favor evidence that supports our existing beliefs, and overlook information that gives us reasons to reconsider. The human, interventionist elements in a robust barrier system depend on people who are able to detect discrepancies and unexpected turns of events. One such element can be that an experienced professional, who usually does exceptionally good work, has an off-day and is about to put people at risk because of a misjudgement of a situation or a lapse in concentration. Knowledge and awareness about these three psychological phenomena, then, are important in designing an organizational climate where people take action when they spot what they perceive to be a mistake.

3 Beyond Hint and Hope

Human intervention is often the most challenging kind of barrier element to put in place. Technology and procedure plans are more concrete and tangible. Creating a work environment where it is normal to voice your concerns is not so straightforward. The essence of the human element in barriers is that people need to speak up when they witness something out of the ordinary, events that startle, surprise, or frighten them. It seems that aviation has managed to make it normal to do so, thus creating a safety culture that other professional disciplines can take inspiration and learn from.

Speaking up when you sense that somebody has made an error or is about to do so, can be particularly hard for a junior person towards a senior person in an organization. A newly employed person may be less prone to the aspect blindness mentioned earlier, and may see things that the veterans in the workplace are unaware of, but also be unsure about whether it is a good and welcome thing to speak up. A way of communication that has been detected in aviation and in healthcare in such circumstances is what has been called hint and hope. A person, who perceives that something is wrong, but is afraid of the consequences of intervening in the situation, may decide to give a hint about his or her observation, and hope that it will be sufficient to generate a positive response. Investigations into accidents in aviation and healthcare have documented a range of hint and hope responses. A nurse sees that the anesthetics doctor is preparing to set a syringe in what she perceives to be the patient's wrong shoulder. They are supposed to perform surgery on the left shoulder, and not the right one that the doctor is now getting ready to treat. The nurse is not completely confident in her judgement, and thus decides to hint rather than say out straight that they are now focusing on the wrong shoulder. Then things happen very quickly, the doctors in charge do not understand the hint, and they cut open the wrong shoulder. In the investigation that takes place after the event, the nurse claims that she tried to tell the doctors about the emerging mistake, while they say that she did try to say something to them, but the message was unclear.

It is understandable that people turn to hint and hope instead of addressing an issue in more direct manner. The motivation for vague and indirect communication can protect both the sender and the receiver from unpleasantness.

> A lot us are taught that it is not polite to confront another person by directly stating a problem, opinion, or disagreement. Hinting and hoping is a communication strategy that courteous people are tempted to use to avoid confrontation, to preserve someone else's sense of dignity or status, or to protect themselves from criticism and rejection. People hint and hope every day. (Gordon, Mendenhall, & O'Connor, 2012, p. 59)

When hint and hope works, it is an elegant form of communication, where you succeed in correcting a person's behavior in other people's presence, without anybody else noticing it. On other occasions, the hinting is a feeble and weak barrier that cannot stop a mistake from creating a horrible outcome. The Tenerife disaster on March 27, 1977, where two Boing 747 airplanes from Pan American and KLM crashed on the runway, killing 583 people, one of the pilots took off before having received clearance to do so. A recording of the conversation inside the KLM plane reveals that the flight engineer hints that the other plan may be in their way. "Is he not clear, that Pan American?" (Weick, 1990). The warning signal he provides to the pilot is not strong enough, so he proceeds to take the plane onto its fatal journey. Here is an example hint and hope as part of a weak barrier system. The pilot makes a mistake, and it starts a causal chain that ends with disaster, since no barriers are in place to prevent it from happening. A steadfast and persistent flight engineer or co-pilot could have made a difference, but none of them dared to confront their senior, who was one of KLM's highest ranked and most respected pilots. The pilot had recently provided the first officer with a qualification check to work in a Boing 747, and that might have contributed to make the threshold for confronting him higher than normal. In his analysis of the accident, Weick (1990, p. 574) comments: "Perhaps influenced by his great prestige making it difficult to imagine an error of this magnitude on the part of such an expert pilot, both the co-pilot and the flight engineer made no further objections."

I witnessed an interesting example of hint and hope during a seminar for leaders in a Norwegian city council. Before the seminar, the administrative leader told me that he wanted to say a few words of truth to the fifty or so participants. He said to me that he was disappointed with the collaboration between them. Individually, they were thinking solely about their own units, and not about what would be best for the city council as a whole. There was little solidarity among them. Now he had the opportunity to confront them and demand improvement.

The leader then took the podium and told the leaders a story about gees, about how they fly together and support each other. Whenever one goose struggles to keep the tempo during flight, two other gees will connect to it and help it to gain speed. Whenever the leader goose is exhausted from flying in the front, another goose will take over, and allow the leader to rest. The audience smiled politely at the story, and that was it. Afterward, I talked to the administrative leader, who was very pleased with himself. "Now I really gave them something to think about." he said, indicating that he thought he had been sharp and direct in pointing out a lack of collaboration amongst the leaders. From my perspective, he had failed in addressing the issue properly. I doubt that any of the leaders noted a critical or challenging note in the story about the geese. It was another example of hint and hope, of fruitless communication based on a wish not to hurt or anger anybody. The incident can also be analyzed in the terms from Reason's barrier model. The administrative leader perceived that the city council leaders were on the wrong path with regard to collaboration and solidarity, and attempted to stop a chain of events ultimately leading to the suboptimal use of public resources, and worse service for the citizens. It was most likely an unsuccessful attempt, since he used hint and hope, rather than direct communication.

In aviation, there has been a quest to move beyond hint and hope, to more direct and unambiguous ways of communication. The Tenerife disaster was a turning point, generating activities to improve feedback quality amongst employees, under the heading of Crew Resource Management (CRM). Gordon, Mendenhall, & O'Connor (2012, p. 59) convey how CRM encourages crew to focus on *what* is right rather than *who* is right, and thus draws attention to the matters of fact rather than on opposing views and rivalry amongst colleagues about who has the most appropriate understanding of the situation. Personal prestige can stand in the way of clarification of the situation at hand, since it makes people hold on to their own beliefs, even beyond the point where they have obtained strong reasons to revise them. CRM is all about challenging each other in respectful manners, with a constructive intention. The person who is expressing a concern should be specific about the content, and timely, not hesitating to speak up at the moment when something appears to be wrong. CRM encourages crew to seek information, ask questions and push for clarification of situations that appear ambiguous to them. In order to be effective, the human dimension of a barrier system depends on a wholehearted commitment to these principles of direct and unambiguous speech.

Flight engineer Morten Theiste conveys an experience where a pilot he was working with needed a reminder about his commitment to CRM (Theiste, 2017). This pilot had trouble with the autopilot in the aircraft on the second last leg of the day. The device had disconnected several times. Even though the crew could reconnect it, the autopilot continued to disconnect. The pilot was looking forward to a short turnaround in Oslo before his last leg to home base in Copenhagen but he had to report the autopilot problem to technical staff in Oslo. He considered it to be a minor issue, and thought that he could easily fly the aircraft manually home and have the Copenhagen technical staff to look at the autopilot during night stop.

"I was called out to meet this crew to check up the matter at the gate after landing. The aircraft had been emptied and was ready for boarding when I came to the gate. The captain explained the problem to me. I said that I needed to go back to the hangar to check the technical manuals about the specific logic behind the autopilot disconnect during the described circumstances. Sometimes an autopilot disconnect may indicate that something more is wrong than just the autopilot itself. When I explained this to the captain, he went totally mad, shouting at me, calling me different ugly names and said he needed the turnaround to be fast so that he could return home to his family. He did not need the autopilot to fly back to Copenhagen. The captain verbally abused me and made me almost speechless. After a while, I simply asked him:—Are you angry with me?" (Theiste, 2017).

This simple question got the pilot to see the situation more clearly, much like the pilot in the situation with the persistent driver of the pushback tractor in the introduction to this book. "I saw in his face that he suddenly was reminded of the CRM training he had been through on how to communicate to each other in the aviation industry. He then realized that he had been acting in an unprofessional manner and that it was a great thing that I took the safety of the passengers seriously and did not immediately release the aircraft" (Theiste, 2017).

An hour later, the aircraft was ready for takeoff, after a thorough investigation of the technical issue with the autopilot. The two professionals at the core of the episode had experienced a critical quality moment, a situation where the flight engineer could have succumbed to the pilot's strong wishes to ignore the technical problem and proceed immediately to takeoff. Verbal abuse from a senior person can easily lead to such a decision from a junior person. It is the kind of behavior that can weaken the will to speak up, and thus can pose a threat to the robustness of a barrier system. In this particular situation, the flight engineer stood his ground, and his reminder to the pilot about the common platform for communicating about safety was enough to diffuse the tension and get the professionals back on track together.

4 Teamwork

One further narrative about barriers and safety illustrates how Reason's model is relevant beyond aviation. It concerns pilot Gimmestad's experience when he went through laser eye surgery. The narrative also highlights the nuances between teamwork and individual expert effort. One surgeon and two nurses were in the operating room with him, and he was awake during the entire two-hour operation. One thing started to worry him as the operation proceeded, and that was the lack of talk around him. The operating room was quiet, with no conversation going on between the three people who were working on his eye. "I have learned the people who work together on complex tasks, should talk with each other, to ensure that things were done in the right manner. In a cockpit, silence is a sign of potential danger. It can mean that something out of the ordinary is going on, and the persons involved are confused or uncertain about what to do." (Gimmestad, 2016) When listening to conversations recorded in cockpits before plane crashes, one striking feature is that the people involved gradually speak less and less to each other. With this knowledge in his mind, Gimmestad found the silence in the operating room disconcerting, and wondered why the surgeon and the two nurses were not speaking to each other.

The operation on Gimmestad's eye went well, so the silence turned out to be a false alarm. Nevertheless, the pilot was curious about the lack of talk, and asked the surgeon about it afterward, explaining that a crucial feature of safety in his own profession was the conversations in the crew. "Who is your co-pilot during an operation?" he asked the surgeon. The response was that the surgeon did not have a person to talk to like that, and did not perceive that he needed one either. It appeared that the surgeon considered himself to be so skillful with his tools that he did not need people around who could correct or challenge him in critical situations. Gimmestad wondered why the nurses could not be involved as conversation partners during an operation, to ensure that things were done in the right order and that mishaps would be spotted and addressed. The surgeon dismissed that idea, claiming that the nurses were not on his level of expertise and experience. The pilot retorted that at least some nurses are experienced, and have participated in many complex operations, gaining knowledge about procedures and possible complications. "That may be true, but they will never be on my level," answered the surgeon (Gimmestad, 2016).

No matter how brilliant the surgeon is in his work, it seems unlikely that he will go through his professional life without making errors that can have dramatic negative effects on patients. With the attitude he expressed in the conversation with Gimmestad, it appears that the barrier system to detect and confront his wrong moves is weak or even nonexistent. A slip, lapse, or mistake from this surgeon is likely to start a causal chain of events that will not stop until a patient has been injured. He seems to perceive himself as an infallible individual, who may need others for assistance and help to keep processes flowing, but not to critically evaluate his decisions and behavior as they happen.

I have discussed this story with experienced healthcare staff, who are critical of the surgeon's apparently dismissive attitude towards the nurses' possible role as dialogue partners during the operation, and towards the need for collaboration and feedback from colleagues. However, they say that one reason for the quiet that concerned Gimmestad can be that the surgeon performed a high precision operation, requiring intense personal concentration to be able to things exactly right. During such a process, talk may be counterproductive. Those moments of deep concentration do not take up the full two-hours process, so can only account for some of the silence the patient encountered.

It has become safer to travel by airplane after a shift from an individualistic to a more team-oriented approach, where it has become normal to challenge the decisions of the pilot, who we no longer consider to see as an infallible superman. Practitioners in healthcare and other parts of organizational life can learn from this development towards non-heroic professionalism. From time to time, stories of heroism still occur in aviation, none more dramatic than when captain Chesley B. Sullenberger on January 15, 2009, landed US Airline Flight 1549 on the Hudson River, after the plane had hit a flock of geese and lost power in both engines. In interviews, Sullenberger has reiterated that the successful landing and subsequent evacuation of the 155 people on board was a team effort, involving the entire crew. Nevertheless, he is the one who gets public attention and hero treatment. One particular detail in the transcript from the cockpit voice recorder indicates that Sullenberger's collaborate mentality is real. His final remark to the co-pilot as they are approaching the water and getting ready for impact is "Got any ideas?" Here is an open invitation to the co-pilot to contribute, and not hold back any suggestions he might have about how to proceed from here. Those three words seem to express personal vulnerability, a realization that they are a team who are in this situation together, and need to draw on their collective resources to get out of it, irrespective of rank and position. Now is the moment to speak up. The co-pilot answers "Actually not", right before impact (Brazy, 2009).

This chapter has presented narratives from aviation, and interpreted them in the light of theoretical approaches to fallibility at work. Research indicates that safety in aviation has improved, and three guiding insights appear to be at the core of this development:

1. All pilots are fallible, including the most skillful and experienced among them.
2. Professionals can be blind to important aspects of their work environment, and they are often blind to this kind of aspect blindness.
3. Safety in aviation depends primarily on teamwork, and not on separate, individual efforts.

Implementation of these insights can happen with the aid of Reason's Swiss Cheese Model. It offers concrete conceptual tools for handling human fallibility. Organizations can use it (a) to create awareness about the importance of voicing intervention, (b) to analyze and critically assess current ability to deal with error, and (c) to get people to take action and voice a concern when they perceive that somebody has made a mistake. The model originated in aviation, but it can be useful in any setting where it is important to identify mistakes and stop them from causing bad outcomes. Barriers can be technological, as when an alarm goes off when somebody has forgotten to do things properly. They can also be procedural, in that people are trained to follow a particular checklist and are thus able to detect the deviations from normal and correct procedures. Human intervention is the third type of barrier, and often the most fragile one, since it requires that people develop habits of speaking up, even when they are deeply uncomfortable about doing so. Hint and hope may be the least confrontational and most courteous strategy, but also one that is likely to fail. In professional settings, we can witness activities that unbeknownst to the agents seem destined to cause havoc, and need to engage in the matter without hesitation, in order to avoid the bad outcome. Doing that takes courage, and may require considerable training and preparation. In organizations, the barrier system will form a part of the culture, of the way things are normally done there. It is a particularly pressing responsibility for leaders to be aware of the strengths and weaknesses of the current barrier system, and to take steps to strengthen and improve it.

References

Bledow, R., Carette, B., Kühnel, J., & Bister, D. (2017). Learning from others' failures: The effectiveness of failure stories for managerial learning. *Academy of Management Learning & Education, 16*(1), 39–53.

Brazy, D. P. (2009). *Cockpit voice recorder DCA9MA026*. Retrieved from Washington, DC: http://www.exosphere3d.com/pubwww/pdf/flight_1549/ntsb_docket/420526.pdf.

Gimmestad, J. (2016, 18th November). *Interviewer: Ø. Kvalnes*.

Gordon, S., Mendenhall, P., & O'Connor, B. B. (2012). *Beyond the checklist: What else health care can learn from aviation teamwork and safety*. Ithaca, NY: Cornell University Press.

Helmreich, R. L., & Davies, J. M. (2004). Culture, threat, and error: Lessons from aviation. *Canadian Journal of Anesthesia, 51*(1), R1–R4.

Kao, L. S., & Thomas, E. J. (2008). Navigating towards improved surgical safety using aviation-based strategies. *Journal of Surgical Research, 145*(2), 327–335.

Kvalnes, Ø. (2010). *Det feilbarlige menneske: Risiko og læring i arbeidslivet*. Oslo: Universitetsforlaget.

Mack, A. (2003). Inattentional blindness. *Current Directions in Psychological Science, 12*(5), 180–184.

Pronovost, P. J., Goeschel, C. A., Olsen, K. L., Pham, J. C., Miller, M. R., Berenholtz, S. M., et al. (2009). Reducing health care hazards: Lessons from the commercial aviation safety team. *Health Affairs, 28*(3), w479–w489.

Rami, U., & Gould, C. (2016). From a "culture of blame" to an encouraged "learning from failure culture". *Business Perspectives & Research, 4*(2), 161–168.

Reason, J. (1990). *Human error*. Cambridge: Cambridge University Press.

Report on the Convair 340 aircraft accident. (1993). Retrieved from http://reports.aviation-safety.net/1989/19890908-0_CVLT_LN-PAA.pdf.

Simons, D. J., & Chabris, C. F. (1999). Gorillas in our midst: Sustained inattentional blindness for dynamic events. *Perception, 28*(9), 1059–1074.

Stoop, J. A., & Kahan, J. P. (2005). Flying is the safest way to travel: How aviation was a pioneer in independent accident investigation. *European Journal of Transport and Infrastructure Research, 5*(2), 115–128.

Theiste, M. (2017, 19th April). *Interviewer: Ø. Kvalnes.*

Weick, K. E. (1990). The vulnerable system: An analysis of the Tenerife air disaster. *Journal of Management, 16*(3), 571–593.

Wilf-Miron, R., Lewenhoff, I., Benyamini, Z., & Aviram, A. (2003). From aviation to medicine: Applying concepts of aviation safety to risk management in ambulatory care. *Quality and Safety in Health Care, 12*(1), 35–39.

Open Access This chapter is licensed under the terms of the Creative Commons Attribution 4.0 International License (http://creativecommons.org/licenses/by/4.0/), which permits use, sharing, adaptation, distribution and reproduction in any medium or format, as long as you give appropriate credit to the original author(s) and the source, provide a link to the Creative Commons license and indicate if changes were made.

The images or other third party material in this chapter are included in the chapter's Creative Commons license, unless indicated otherwise in a credit line to the material. If material is not included in the chapter's Creative Commons license and your intended use is not permitted by statutory regulation or exceeds the permitted use, you will need to obtain permission directly from the copyright holder.

5

Fallibility and Trust in Healthcare

"It was total paralysis, and every birth doctor's worst nightmare, to find that your own mistake caused the death of a baby. It is a horrible tragedy for the parents, but also a nightmare for the staff at the hospital. I remember when the father looked me in the eyes and asked me why we did not perform a caesarean birth. My reply was that I had made a mistake, and not read the journal properly. If we had followed the original plan, the baby would most probably have lived" (Westad, 2016).

Stian Westad is the head doctor of the women's clinic at Lillehammer Hospital in Norway. Some years ago, he experienced how a mistake on the part of him and his team caused the death of a baby. The pregnant woman was expecting her first child. The time of expected conception was coming close, and the woman was anxious, because her stomach was so big. She went to the hospital, and the ultrasound showed that she was expecting a big child. In the journal, the doctor wrote that if the birth had not started by itself within one week, they would proceed to perform a caesarean birth. When the woman returned to the hospital some time later, a new ultrasound was taken, and this time the conclusion was that the child was not so big after all. That turned out to be a fatally mistaken change of view. When the birth started, the doctor decided for a vaginal rather than a caesarean birth. The baby was stuck during the birth, suffered severe brain damage, and died four weeks later.

"The baby would have survived if we had stayed with the original plan, and kept the promise to the parents of performing a caesarean if the birth did not start normally. I feel that we owe it to the parents and the child who died to not hide this away, but speak openly about it, so that we can use it constructively and improve. I told the parents instantly that we, the hospital staff, had made a mistake and that they had done things exactly right" (Westad, 2016). The doctor remained in contact with the parents, and when the woman became pregnant again, they chose to have the same doctor and the same midwife to follow them up. The hospital crew's openness about their mistake created trust, and this time the process ended as expected, with the birth of a healthy baby.

In the aftermath of the mistake, Westad received support from colleagues, and together they critically scrutinized procedures to strengthen them, to minimize the risk of making the same mistake again. He hopes that his openness will make others come forward and talk about their mistakes. "When we have made a mistake, we have a unique opportunity to improve. If we ignore the mistakes we have made, we are at risk of repeating them, and that would be unforgivable" (Westad, 2016).

This chapter discusses examples from healthcare, both to illustrate further the relevance of the concepts from previous chapters, and to introduce the concept of trust into the discussion about fallibility. Hospital staff face situations where it is important that they voice a concern, and intervene to stop chains of events that may lead to unnecessary injury or death. Hospitals and other organizations in the health sector need to create a barrier system where people do not hesitate to voice their concerns, a communication climate where it is normal and appreciated to intervene when you sense that something is wrong.

The guiding ideas of this chapter are that openness about mistakes (i) can serve a foundation for trust within a professional unit, (ii) is necessary for further learning and improvement of professional services, and (iii) can strengthen public trust in the service providers. Trust will be understood as a function of ability, benevolence, and integrity (Mayer, Davis, & Schoorman, 1995; Schoorman, Mayer, & Davis, 2007). Trust can be one of the pathways for building high-quality connections at work (Dutton, 2003; Dutton & Heaphy, 2003). The examples in the current chapter illustrate how open talk about failures and mistakes can serve to build, maintain, and even repair trust, and also how a climate for such exchanges needs to be characterized by psychological safety (Carmeli, Brueller, & Dutton, 2009; Edmondson, 1999). What is at stake is also organizational trust (Schoorman, Mayer, & Davis, 1996). Hospitals and other health organizations need to display a willingness and ability to learn from failure in order to be deemed trustworthy by the public. The main data for this chapter comes from interviews with two experienced doctors. Both exemplify a growth mindset (Dweck, 2017) in that they see situations where things go wrong as an opportunity to learn and improve their professional work, individually and in teams.

1   Immediate Acknowledgement

Doctor Westad explains that his motivation for being open about his mistake in not initiating a caesarean birth was the thought that there is good health in doing the right thing immediately. He quickly erased any tendency on the parents' side to think that they should have done things differently, that the death of their baby had even the slightest to do with any miscalculations from their side. In the light of other dramatic incidents where mistakes lead to bad outcomes, this immediacy seems important. If you hesitate and do not admit a mistake at the beginning, it might become more difficult later, since you then have to explain two things, both the mistake itself, and the fact that you did not speak up about it on the first occasion where that was possible.

Failure to admit mistakes early can create long and painful processes of denying and attributing blame. One dramatic example is the Hillsborough disaster in Sheffield on April 15, 1989, where 96 supporters were crushed to death at a football match (Scraton, 1999, 2016). It was not until April 2016 that an inquest returned a verdict that the supporters died due to grossly negligent failures by police and ambulance services to fulfill their duty of care to the supporters (Scraton, 2016). For twenty-seven years, the professionals had denied any mistakes, and had instead explained the tragedy as a result of reckless behavior from the supporters themselves. Families and friends endured the extra pain of these speculations and accusations. Doing the right thing immediately, as exemplified by doctor Westad's response to his own mistake, would have made an immensely positive difference to a great number of people, over a long period of time. It may not have been necessary to take full and unconditional responsibility, but admitting a considerable part of the blame for the tragic events would no doubt have made a significant positive difference for many people.

It is worthwhile to dwell on the idea that there is good health to doing the right thing immediately after a mistake. It is a move that punctures any tendency towards a blame game, the kind of process we have seen after the Hillsborough tragedy. In hospital settings, a blame game often develops in the aftermath of shocking and publicly exposed mistakes. From time to time, in different cultures and settings, an operating team forgets a scissor inside a patient's stomach. When the patient returns to the hospital in great pain, and professionals detect the mistake, the game of attributing personal blame can begin. The head surgeon may blame the nurse in charge of counting the number of instruments. She should have noted the missing instrument, and stopped the process of sewing the operation wound. The doctor himself can deny responsibility for the unfortunate turn of events. A surgeon is normally so preoccupied with the complex and difficult operation tasks that it is impossible for him or her to keep track of all the instruments that are in use. It is common that not only one, but two nurses have it as their main responsibility to count the instruments and speak up when one or more go missing. Nevertheless, when things do go wrong, the surgeon can decide to take responsibility on behalf of the team, and not point a blaming finger at one or two colleagues. A heated and public blame game can create an impression of an unprofessional and divided workplace, characterized by unhealthy individual strife rather than a team-oriented organization where colleagues shared the responsibility in the face of misadventure. Dutton (2003, p. 97) has noted how public chastising of people for poor performances is sometimes seen as a necessary way of being tough, but is also likely to be a "trust killer", corroding professional relationships at work.

We can attempt to generalize from Westad's behavior to a principle for professionals to follow in situations similar to the one he faced, highlighting the quality of immediacy in the response.

Principle of immediate acknowledgement: When you realize that your decision or behavior has caused harm, admit it and take responsibility immediately.

In the critical aftermath of a bad outcome, victims can be particularly susceptible to blaming themselves, no matter how irrational that may seem. When the professional meets them very early with an acknowledgement of responsibility, that causal attribution is much less likely to happen. One important dimension of the current example is that Westad could immediately grasp the facts of the situation, including his team's role in bringing about the terrible outcome. In other situations, doctors, nurses, and other healthcare workers may be under pressure to acknowledge that they have made a fatal mistake, but may need more time to evaluate the circumstances and their own contribution to the outcome. The pressure to admit a mistake may also be present in situations where a reasonable interpretation of the facts does not warrant such an act. Angry and frustrated patients or relatives may understandably push for it, even in cases where the healthcare workers have actually done excellent work, to no avail. Those kinds of cases, and how they differ from the ones where the connection between a failure and a bad outcome can be established quickly will be discussed further in the next section.

Doctor Westad stayed in close contact with the parents after the death of their baby, and when the couple expected another baby, they decided to keep the same team of professionals that had helped them the first time. That trust appears to have been built on the foundation of the immediacy of the acknowledgement. Trust can be explained in terms of three factors that need to be in place in relation between the trustor and the trustee (Mayer et al., 1995; Schoorman et al., 1996). The trustor must perceive that the trustee has the necessary ability, benevolence, and integrity to be trustworthy. This understanding of the phenomenon overlaps with Dutton's, who also highlights benevolence and integrity, but uses the more general term of dependability (honesty and reliability) instead of ability (Dutton, 2003, p. 81). The former definition will be used here, since the concept of ability brings forth the non-moral dimension of trust. The trustor must perceive the trustee to have a set of skills and competencies that enables him or her to perform specific tasks. Benevolence is present when the trustor perceives the trustee to be a person who cares about his or her well-being, and gives priority to the trustor's interest over his or her egocentric interest. The trustor sees integrity in the trustee when it seems that the trustee believes in and adheres to a set of principles that the trustor finds acceptable. All three factors must be in place for trust to happen. The absence of any one of them creates an imbalance. It does not help to have ability, if the trustor doubts your benevolence or integrity, and neither of those two factors, together or alone, will suffice as a foundation for trust without being tied to a proper ability.

A fatal mistake at a hospital can create a deep crisis in the trustworthiness the patient (trustor) sees in the professionals (trustees). All the three factors can come under serious doubt, and the trust collapses if one or more of them gives way. It may appear that the doctor or the midwife did not have the necessary abilities to do the job well. Their benevolence can also be questioned. Are they more concerned about themselves than they are about the patient? A mistake with a terrible outcome can also make the patient doubt the integrity of the professionals, and question whether they are really adhering to the right set of principles.

Immediate acknowledgement of a mistake can keep trust alive, or at least create conditions from which to rebuild it. Being open about a mistake is a particularly strong expression of benevolence, in that the professional places the interest of the parents ahead of his own self-interest. Westad could have remained vague about the causes of the baby's death, and even suggested some kind of fatal involvement or lack of proper care from the parents. That would have protected his own narrowly construed professional reputation, and placed more of the burden on the mother and father, who would have lacked the medical expertise to challenge that account. Westad instead chose to prioritize the parents' wellbeing. In doing so, he practiced the benevolence at the core of professional ethics of any kind, as outlined by Nanda (2002), who sees the relation between professional and client or patient as one governed by a more or less explicit pledge from the professional: "Trust me; although my self-interest may dictate other actions, I undertake to serve in your best interest." There can be conflicts of interest, and those situations are distinct from ethical dilemmas, where there are strong ethical reasons to do both A and B, and no matter what you do, something will be wrong. In conflicts of interest, there are strong ethical reasons to prioritize the client or patient, but the professional might be tempted to set his or her self-interest first. That temptation can be particularly strong due to the fact that there is usually a considerable knowledge gap between the provider and receiver of a professional service. The patient has seldom any way of knowing whether the doctor is doing the right thing, or not.

The parents whose baby died decided to use doctor Westad and his team when the next pregnancy occurred. That is a particularly powerful expression of trust. Mayer et al. (1995, pp. 712–714) understand trust as a willingness to be vulnerable. You are willing to trust someone, and assume that they have the required ability, benevolence, and integrity to do the work. That assumption may turn out to be false, and you lose, particularly if you engage in actual, trusting actions. Mayer et al. (1995, p. 724) distinguish between trust and trusting activities, and only the latter are truly risky. You can have a willingness to be vulnerable without ever becoming engaged in any risky activity, because the occasion never arises. The parents in question did both, in that the willingness was in place, and led to the concrete trusting action of staying with the professional team whose mistake had caused their first baby's death. They must have had a strong belief along all three dimensions of trust in doctor Westad and his team, despite the tragic outcome of the first pregnancy. It seems that a crucial building block for that trust was Westad's immediate acknowledgement of responsibility. The parents could go through a grief process without being tormented by thoughts about personal responsibility, and about how they could have done things differently to save the baby.

Admitting the mistake generated trust between doctor Westad and the parents. It is also likely that this act of honesty also contributed to a trusting environment at the doctor's unit, and so to a strengthening of professional connections. When the leader steps forward and talks openly about what he did wrong, it lowers the threshold for others to do the same, and also signals the presence of ability, benevolence, and integrity at the top of the professional unit.

2 Barriers in Healthcare

Mistakes in medicine and healthcare is a considerable source of harm to patients even in countries where the professionals are well educated and trained. One study indicates that medical error is the third most common cause of death in the US (Makary & Daniel, 2016). In the previous chapter, we saw how a safety culture in aviation rests on the assumption that human beings are fallible. Even the most experienced professionals are prone to fail, and that creates a need for a system to detect their mistakes before they lead to harmful outcomes. Human intervention is a crucial element in any barrier system, as it can stop the causal chain of events set in motion by a professional's mistake.

Doctor Westad was asked about what he thought could make a doctor hesitate about telling others about his or her mistake at work. One aspect he drew attention to was that of social cost. "A doctor may think that colleagues will see him as a loser if he admits to a mistake" (Westad, 2016). There is a parallel here to the perceived social cost of asking a colleague for help. That, too, is an initiative people tend to perceive to be socially costly. You risk losing face at work if you ask for help and are open about the limitations to your own competence. Brooks, Gino, and Schweitzer (2015) have studied the assumption that people who ask for help are considered to be less competent than those who try to manage on their own, and their data suggest the opposite. When work tasks are complex, the person who asks help for is seen as more competent than the one who do not. The relation between fallibility and asking for help at work will be explored further in Chap. 6.

Another aspect Westad drew attention to is that many young doctors are on temporary work contracts. They may want to be perceived as reliable and infallible professionals, in order to get a permanent job at the hospital. That ambition may also cause them to hold back when they are witness to mistakes and mishaps in the making in the hospital. They may decide to keep silent, out of a wish of not becoming an unpopular figure among the senior, permanently employed doctors, who will have a say in whether they get a contract renewal or even permanent employment. They do not perceive speaking up as a good career move.

Doctor Bjørn Atle Bjørnbeth is an experienced gastro surgeon at Oslo University Hospital. We have discussed communication climate and fallibility at work on a number of occasion in the past fifteen years. His experiences in sharing narratives about mistakes are the focal point of the next section. Even he identifies these career considerations as a major obstacle to openness about mistakes in a hospital, both to reporting about one's own and those of colleagues (Bjørnbeth, 2017). From a leadership perspective, it is possible to neutralize both of these reasons for holding back when witnessing something out of the ordinary, by inviting people to voice their concerns, and by rewarding those who actually do.

Westad and Bjørnbeth are both concerned about how social cost and threat to career development can weaken the barrier system at a hospital. As noted in Chap. 4, Reason's model starts from the assumption that people are fallible, and that each mistake they do start a causal chain of events that leads to a bad outcome, unless there is a barrier in place to bring that chain of events to an earlier stop. Human intervention is one possible barrier element, and the more people experience that the voicing of a concern will be valued and appreciated in the organization, the more likely it is that the will actually do so.

In order to investigate the two experienced doctors' thoughts about how young doctors may be reluctant to speak up about mistakes, I interviewed doctor student Arne (not his real name) about his experiences when being exposed to hospital work for the first time. One of the episodes he shared exemplifies an attempt to voice a concern and function as the human element in a barrier system:

> I was present when a doctor was doing a Nasopharynx test, where the aim is to get a microbiological sample from a specific location 6 to 8 centimeters into the nose cavity. The sample can tell us what kind of airway infection the patient has, and will determine what kind of treatment to

> pursue. The instrument is a brush, similar to a q-tip, but thinner and longer. I noticed that the doctor only inserted the instrument a few millimeters into the nostrils, and took samples there, where the microbiological flora is different. At school, we had learned that this is a mistake. Not only will the test be useless, but also the result can potentially mislead the doctor into making faulty decisions about treatment. I let the doctor know after the patient had left the room. (Arne, 2016)

The doctor had made a mistake, and the student took an initiative to stop the causal chain of events it put in motion. As such, the student behaved in an exemplary manner. The doctor, however, did not see things that way:

> In response, he got mad at me, and said that I was supposed to learn from him, and not the other way around. Anyway, I hope he took in what I said and corrected his understanding of the test for later, because what he did was completely wrong, a bit like making a blood analysis of a urine sample. (Arne, 2016)

Without claiming that the situation above is typical, it is at least a stark example of the concrete circumstances where the communication climate between seniors and juniors in a work environment is put to the test. Arne's own interpretation was that the more experienced doctor found it socially difficult to be confronted with a mistake by a junior. Here was an opportunity to strengthen the climate for making such interventions, by thanking the junior for the effort, in line with what the pilot did in his meeting with the driver of the pushback tractor, in the example from the introduction of this book. That opportunity was not taken, but at least we can share the hope expressed by the student that the doctor actually absorbed the information and silently revised his understanding of how to perform the test.

Conveying feedback in a constructive way is often easier said than done, particularly for a junior in relation to a senior. It can be a challenge in a range of professional setting, also beyond healthcare. In an interview, finance student Mina Randjelovic explained a strategy she used towards a senior colleague during a work assignment in a company. The two were supposed to have an expert—apprentice relationship, much as in the case of the senior doctor and the doctor student mentioned above. From time to time, the senior would make a mistake in preparing a particular business document, and the junior would catch it. "In those situations, I said to him that what he just did was really interesting, and I asked him to explain why he had done it. That way he had to rethink his behavior, and was able to detect and correct the mistake himself" (Randjelovic, 2017). She cleverly spared her colleague of the potential humiliation of being corrected by someone less experienced and knowledgeable than he was. Its strategy has a trace of hint and hope to it, and can fail if the recipient is inattentive and slow in his pedagogical effort. A plan B may be needed if the senior is unable to detect his own mistake even after revisiting the faulty reasons for his decision.

The three psychological phenomena highlighted in Chap. 2 can also pose a threat to the robustness of the barrier system in a hospital setting. First, a doctor or nurse can be susceptible to the sunk-cost fallacy, in that he or she has invested professional pride or other currency in one particular way of doing things. The idea of failure may cause cognitive dissonance, a pain that can be held at bay by continuing in the same direction, even with a vague idea that something is not quite right. A turnaround can also require the professional to admit that resources have been wasted, something he or she may be reluctant to do.

Second, there may be a bystander effect, in that many employees are present when the mistake happens, and they have a pacifying effect on each other, a diffusion of responsibility. Each of twenty in a group of doctors and nurses will tend to think that they only have one twentieth of a responsibility to intervene. Furthermore, pluralistic ignorance can occur. Each of the twenty may watch out for a response from the other nineteen, and if those remain passive, each will be prone to think that everything is fine, since none of the others take steps to intervene. Each individual can doubt his or her own initial thought that something is about to go wrong, given that there is no sign of a response from any of the others.

Third, the confirmation fallacy may cause professionals in a hospital to overlook and fail to spot obvious missteps from a colleague. The doctors and nurses who have the status of being the best and most experienced are particularly vulnerable to being allowed to continue on erroneous paths, since their colleagues may interpret whatever they do in the best possible light. They are, after all, the experts in their field. One patient story can serve to convey this situation. A woman was admitted to hospital with a broken ankle, from a skiing accident. The doctor in charge told her that it was an uncomplicated break, and it would even be fine to walk with the plastered foot on the next day. When the woman tried to do so on the following afternoon, it did not go well. It hurt to put the broken foot down on the floor, and the plaster did not seem to give sufficient support for standing or walking. The woman decided to go back to the hospital to explain the problem. One doctor and two nurses listened to her, and inspected the plastered foot. They agreed that it did not look right, and that the plaster should be removed and replaced by a new one. Before they proceeded to do so, the doctor asked who had put on the original plaster, and the patient answered doctor A. That changed the whole interpretation. "Doctor A is the best orthopedist in the Nordic countries. If he has put on the plaster, then it is supposed to be that way." The decision to change plaster was revoked immediately, in the light of who had produced the initial one.

Some weeks after this event, the woman returned to the hospital to have the plaster removed. The doctor in charge assumed that she had already been to take an x-ray to confirm that the break had healed properly. The patient explained that she had been told that this was such an uncomplicated break that no x-ray was needed. "That is very odd. We are always supposed to check that the break has healed before we remove plaster. Whoever said otherwise?" he asked. Again, the patient said that it was doctor A. For the second time, this answer made any misgivings from the professional disappear. "If doctor A says so, it is correct. He is the best orthopedist in the Nordic countries."

This patient twice experienced that professionals put preliminary evaluations of her situations aside because the doctor in charge was renowned for being the best in his field. Special rules applied to him, or he could allow himself to break the rules that ordinary medical workers must follow. The patient's ankle has healed properly, so the medical treatment she got appears to have been right. However, we can have some doubts about the barrier system at the unit where doctor A works.

It appears that everything he does is interpreted in the best possible way, since he is the best orthopedist in the Nordic countries. He is probably an excellent doctor, but the barrier system around him may be weak, in that colleagues commit the confirmation fallacy, assuming that everything he does is correct.

The pilot Jarle Gimmestad has talked of a similar vulnerability among the highest ranked pilots. Juniors and less experienced co-pilots hesitate to intervene when they sense that the seniors are about to make a mistake, often out of reverence to experience, but also for similar reasons as the junior doctors on temporary contracts. It may not be a wise career move to challenge a person who has the power to influence your professional prospects. A senior who is aware of this possible weakness in the barrier system can counter it by encouraging the junior to intervene when he or she notices something out of the ordinary in what the more experienced person is doing (Gimmestad, 2016).

3   Sharing Mistakes

One thing that surprised doctor Westad when he started to talk openly about his mistake was how unique and uncommon this kind of sharing appeared to be. The Norwegian Board of Health Supervision got his and the parents' permission to use it in their annual report, and that led to media interest and invitations for the doctor to give presentations to healthcare workers about the processes before and after the mistake. This attention indicates that it is quite unusual to speak openly about one's mistakes in the health sector in Norway, and that there is room for more learning from them among doctors, nurses, and other healthcare workers.

Interviews with doctor Bjørn Atle Bjørnbeth have focused on his experiences with fallibility at work, and the links between being open about one's mistakes and learning to become a better professional. His initial response to doctor Westad's act of immediate acknowledgement is that it was a very commendable thing to do, but also that many situations where things go wrong in connection with an operation are very complex. It may not be clear-cut that the negative outcome is a result of faulty professional work. An immediate acknowledgement of responsibility may be what the patient or the relatives are want to hear, but the rationale for giving one may not be present. "Prior to an operation, I try to be open about risk to the patients. Sometimes it is difficult to make a precise diagnosis, and we have to proceed without reliable knowledge about what is actually the matter with the patient. The uncertainty means that things might go wrong. Sometimes we operate people for an illness where it is common that about 30% experience more or less serious complications after the operation, and may have to be re-operated. Patients who end up in that category may respond with anger, and expect me to acknowledge a mistake. It would be wrong of me to do that, since we cannot establish whether the current problem is a result of a professional mistake in diagnosing or operating the patient, or not. Absorbing and acknowledging information about risk is difficult for patients and relatives, particularly in the light of a bad outcome" (Bjørnbeth, 2017).

Doctor Bjørnbeth has focused on the learning potential of sharing experiences about unexpected complications and mistakes. One episode from his early career set him on the path to understanding the importance of transparency about fallibility. He was on duty at a hospital when a young girl entered as a patient, with symptoms indicating a broken arm. When studying the x-ray of the arm, doctor Bjørnbeth could not see any break. In order to be on the safe side, he knocked on the door of his leader, the chief doctor of his unit, and showed him the x-ray. The senior doctor studied the picture carefully, and came to the same verdict as young doctor Bjørnbeth. The girl had not broken her arm, and could return home without treatment.

Later on the same day, another doctor came to the unit, and looked at the x-ray of the girl's arm. After careful scrutiny, he spotted a break that was difficult to detect, and had escaped both doctor Bjørnbeth and the chief doctor's gaze. The girl was sent for again, and this time got the proper treatment in the form of plaster.

The next day, doctor Bjørnbeth took the x-ray back to the chief doctor's office, and said that the two of them had missed the break in the girl's arm yesterday. The chief doctor asked to see the picture again, and once more studied it carefully. Then he exclaimed. "Yes, of course there is a break in this arm, but this is not the same picture that you showed me yesterday. I would not have failed to spot something so obvious."

Doctor Bjørnbeth's trust in his leader diminished after this exchange. It was not primarily the belief in the chief doctor's professional abilities that disappeared, but more the perception of his benevolence and integrity. This man appeared to prioritized self-interest over the interest of his younger subordinate, and seemed to adhere to dubious principles regarding leadership support. From a moral luck perspective, we may say that he was unfortunate to encounter circumstances that revealed a weakness of character, a lack of substantial leadership capabilities.

Early in his career, doctor Bjørnbeth became convinced that talk about professional mistakes and failures could be a source of deep and profound learning, making it safer to be a patient at a hospital. In tandem with another young doctor, he initiated a new point on the agenda of the weekly unit meeting: Where have we had unexpected complications this week? In which cases have we failed to diagnose and treat patients faultlessly? The idea was to bring up examples where there would be room for strengthening common and individual work procedures and methods. Both doctors exemplified a growth mindset, an assumption that it is possible to strengthen professional capabilities by dwelling on unforeseen complications and failures (Dweck, 2017). In the beginning, the two initiators took turns in explaining to their colleagues how they had failed in giving perfect treatment to patients, and how they thought things could be done better. "The more experienced doctors listened in, shook their heads in more or less real disbelief at what we, the young colleagues told them. They indicated that such events would never have occurred on their watch. The veterans remained silent about their own mistakes. When their patients had complications after an operation, these doctors would explain that in terms of bad luck. They tended to be surprised whenever things went wrong, having expected that their superior professional efforts would lead to a good outcome" (Bjørnbeth, 2017). These veterans appear to have had a fixed mindset (Dweck, 2017), considering their own capabilities to be fully developed and set in stone. After a while, doctor Bjørnbeth and his equally open colleague decided to terminate this point on the meeting agenda, since nobody else stepped forward to share examples of situations where they had failed to be perfect doctors.

Concepts from attribution theory (Harvey, Madison, Martinko, Crook, & Crook, 2014; Heider, 1958) are useful for making sense of the responses from the doctors who denied fallibility and appealed to bad luck in order to explain bad outcomes. People tend to have an innate interest in understanding the causes of their own and others' successes and failures. An agent's self-attributions can be internal, pointing to individual efforts and skills, or external, pointing to factors beyond the agent's control. As mentioned in Chap. 1, a football coach can explain his team's success in a cup final to be a result of "world class coaching", and thus engage in internal attribution, and a loss in a crucial game as down to bad refereeing or injuries to his own players, applying an external attribution strategy. Learning from failure depends on a realistic balance between internal and external attribution. That appeared to be absent in the case of the veteran doctors who refused to participate in a talk about failures. When you say that bad luck was the sole explanation for a negative outcome, you also indicate that you have nothing to learn from carefully studying the case at hand, inviting colleagues to evaluate your work, and to consider whether you could have done things differently. In the case of a successful outcome, the tendency to engage in internal attribution, explaining it primarily to be a result of individual expertise and effort can also hamper learning, in that fortunate dimensions of the situation are ignored. The shift in self-understanding in the light of success and failure can also be interpreted as a move from understanding oneself as an agent, to understanding oneself as a mere pawn (Nygård, 2007).

Attribution error happens when a person over- or underestimates his or her own contribution to a particular outcome (Ross, Amabile, & Steinmetz, 1977). Doctor Westad's immediate acknowledgement of responsibility appears to have been motivated by a wish to prevent the parents from committing the attribution error of taking part of the blame for the baby's death.

A relevant development in research on attribution has been to move beyond the distinction between internal and external, to include relational attribution in explanations of outcomes (Eberly, Holley, Johnson,

& Mitchell, 2011). The success or failure of interpersonal interactions in organizations often depends on the quality of the teamwork, a dimension not properly captured in the traditional dualistic model of attribution theory. Dialogue between colleagues about recent failures can serve to utilize and strengthen the relational dimension at work.

In recent years, doctor Bjørnbeth has been the leader of a large unit at the Oslo University Hospital. When he took over responsibility as leader, work environment surveys indicated weaknesses in the communication climate. Regular exchanges of harsh words created a climate where people dreaded to go to work. Fallibility was at the core of the troubles, in that some doctors found it difficult to accept that even they could make mistakes, and might depend upon colleagues to intervene. Based on a series of one-on-one employee conversations, doctor Bjørnbeth gradually identified the challenges and set new standards for communication at the unit. A stronger team mentality emerged, where it was considered normal to voice a concern and engage in constructive criticism. The individuals who had contributed negatively to the work environment through harsh language were able to engage more respectfully in conversations with colleagues (Bjørnbeth, 2017).

One fixed agenda feature at the unit currently led by doctor Bjørnbeth is a meeting where they go through complications and unexpected developments from the past week. It is a version of the same kind of meeting his colleague and he tried and failed to establish years earlier. "At a recent meeting, we discussed a case where the operation itself had gone well, but there had been more blood than expected. I had cut a hole in a blood vessel, and had failed to anticipate the amount of blood that would come out of it, creating a more stressful situation than foreseen. We could have avoided that with a more careful look at the x-ray. We learned that for operations of that kind, we need to look more closely at the size of the closest blood vessels" (Bjørnbeth, 2017).

Sharing mistakes and talking openly about them require the presence of high-quality relationships between colleagues, and thus a sense of psychological safety (Carmeli et al., 2009; Edmondson, 1999). When colleagues sit down to talk about their experiences of not getting things right, they expose themselves to criticism and even humiliation. It is only in a work environment perceived to be psychologically safe that participants are likely to talk openly about tasks they have struggled with.

Dutton (2003) has noted how we can build trust in a work environment by being open about weaknesses: "Disclosing something of ourselves—especially information that makes us vulnerable in some way—is an especially powerful way to convey and generate trust." Doctors and nurses who speak openly to one another about mistakes assume that nobody will use the information they share against them at a later stage, and so take a risk. The assumption may be false, and a colleague may betray the trust by exposing the information in some other setting. One reason why it can be difficult to create trust in a work environment is that people are not ready to make themselves vulnerable. Instead, they adopt a wait-and-see attitude or a "show me" stance (Dutton, 2003, p. 82). You go first, and then I might join you afterward. In the previous, unsuccessful attempt to create a practice of sharing mistakes, nobody was willing to follow in the footsteps of Bjørnbeth and his colleague. In Bjørnbeth's current workplace, on the other hand, a system of trust appears to be in place, creating what Dutton sees as the potential for gradual strengthening of that attitude: "When we take the first step in building trust, we become crafters of connecting possibilities. Rather than passively waiting to see whether someone can be trusted, we actively start the virtuous cycle in which trust builds on itself" (Dutton, 2003, p. 82). Here we have a procedure for countering a tendency to hold back, of taking an initiative to break with the attitude of not being open about one's own mistakes because you do not expect others to be equally open.

The main examples and input in this chapter have been from healthcare, where there is a potential to create trust and learn to become better professionals by being open about mistakes and failures. Doctor Westad's open acknowledgement of his mistake created an opportunity for him and his colleagues to learn and to improve their professional work with pregnant women. Other doctors, nurses, and midwives in the same line of work can also take note of what went wrong in that particular case, and adjust their own efforts accordingly. It is also striking how the idea that there is much health in immediate acknowledgement of a mistake, is relevant in other contexts where the things go wrong and victims may start to question their own decision-making and conduct. Dutton has identified trust as one of the pathways to high-quality connections at work, and doctor Westad's conduct appears to have generated trust both in relation to patients and among colleagues. Input from doctor Bjørnbeth indicates that there are also more complex cases, where a doctor needs to withstand pressure to take full responsibility for a bad outcome. His experience also points in the direction of sharing mistakes and analyzing them together as a powerful way of improving one's professional work. The concepts of internal, external, and relational attribution can also be useful in sorting out the causes of good and bad outcomes of interpersonal interactions at work. The next chapter will investigate the more specific topic of normalizing acts of seeking and offering help as a fruitful way to cope with fallibility at work.

References

Arne, S. (2016, 10th December). *Interview with student Arne/Interviewer: Ø. Kvalnes.*
Bjørnbeth, B. A. (2017, 18th January). *Interviewer: Ø. Kvalnes.*
Brooks, A. W., Gino, F., & Schweitzer, M. E. (2015). Smart people ask for (my) advice: Seeking advice boosts perceptions of competence. *Management Science, 61*(6), 1421–1435.
Carmeli, A., Brueller, D., & Dutton, J. E. (2009). Learning behaviours in the workplace: The role of high-quality interpersonal relationships and psychological safety. *Systems Research and Behavioral Science, 26*(1), 81–98.
Dutton, J. E. (2003). *Energize your workplace: How to create and sustain high-quality connections at work.* New York: Wiley.
Dutton, J. E., & Heaphy, E. D. (2003). The power of high-quality connections. *Positive Organizational Scholarship: Foundations of a New Discipline, 3*, 263–278.
Dweck, C. (2017). *Mindset: Changing the way you think to fulfill your potential.* London: Hachette UK.
Eberly, M. B., Holley, E. C., Johnson, M. D., & Mitchell, T. R. (2011). Beyond internal and external: A dyadic theory of relational attribution. *Academy of Management Review, 36*(4), 731–753.

Edmondson, A. (1999). Psychological safety and learning behavior in work teams. *Administrative Science Quarterly, 44*(2), 350–383.

Gimmestad, J. (2016, 18th November). *Interviewer: Ø. Kvalnes.*

Harvey, P., Madison, K., Martinko, M., Crook, T. R., & Crook, T. A. (2014). Attribution theory in the organizational sciences: The road traveled and the path ahead. *Academy of Management Perspectives, 28*(2), 128–146.

Heider, F. (1958). *The psychology of interpersonal relations.* Hoboken, NJ: Wiley.

Makary, M. A., & Daniel, M. (2016). Medical error—The third leading cause of death in the US. *British Medical Journal, 353.*

Mayer, R. C., Davis, J. H., & Schoorman, F. D. (1995). An integrative model of organizational trust. *Academy of Management Review, 20*(3), 709–734.

Nanda, A. (2002). *The essence of professionalism: Managing conflict of interest.* Division of Research, Harvard Business School.

Nygård, R. (2007). *Aktør eller brikke: Søkelys på menneskers selvforståelse.* Oslo Cappelen Damm.

Randjelovic, M. (2017, 17th Februrary). *Interviewer: Ø. Kvalnes.*

Ross, L. D., Amabile, T. M., & Steinmetz, J. L. (1977). Social roles, social control, and biases in social-perception processes. *Journal of Personality and Social Psychology, 35*(7), 485–494.

Schoorman, F. D., Mayer, R. C., & Davis, J. H. (1996). Organizational trust: Philosophical perspectives and conceptual definitions. *Academy of Management Review, 21*(2), 337–340.

Schoorman, F. D., Mayer, R. C., & Davis, J. H. (2007). An integrative model of organizational trust: Past, present, and future. *Academy of Management Review, 32*(2), 344–354.

Scraton, P. (1999). Policing with contempt: The degrading of truth and denial of justice in the aftermath of the Hillsborough disaster. *Journal of Law and Society, 26*(3), 273–297.

Scraton, P. (2016). *Hillsborough—The Truth.* New York: Random House.

Westad, S. (2016, 14th December). *Interviewer: Ø. Kvalnes.*

Open Access This chapter is licensed under the terms of the Creative Commons Attribution 4.0 International License (http://creativecommons.org/licenses/by/4.0/), which permits use, sharing, adaptation, distribution and reproduction in any medium or format, as long as you give appropriate credit to the original author(s) and the source, provide a link to the Creative Commons license and indicate if changes were made.

The images or other third party material in this chapter are included in the chapter's Creative Commons license, unless indicated otherwise in a credit line to the material. If material is not included in the chapter's Creative Commons license and your intended use is not permitted by statutory regulation or exceeds the permitted use, you will need to obtain permission directly from the copyright holder.

6

Approaches to Help in Organizations

The river Akerselva runs through Oslo, from north to south, forming a boundary between the east and the west parts of the city. On hot summer days, the river is a popular place to cool down with a bath or go for a swim. People of all ages can normally enter the river and enjoy the water, but sometimes the current is too strong, and the city council advises people to stay on the shore. There are always a few people who nevertheless decide to enter the river. They are usually strong, athletic types, who are able to look after themselves, and have the muscles and energy to go in and out of the strong current.

A few years ago, there was a noteworthy incident at one of the most popular bathing spots along the river. It was one of those days with a strong current, where most people lay on the shore instead of stepping into the river. A young man was standing in the middle of the river, at the top of a small waterfall. It is usually a comfortable place to stand, facing away from the waterfall, with water gliding at and past you at breast height, but on this day, the stream was faster and more forceful than usual.

From time to time, the man would move towards the shore, and then walk backwards to the spot by the waterfall again. He kept standing there, and people were starting to leave the bathing place for the day. Now it started to look odd that the young man was still standing out in the river, with water rushing at and past him. Somebody shouted out to him: Do you need help? He responded very quickly with a muted confirmation. Yes, he really needed help. This young, athletic man was stuck in the river with its strong current, and had been so for some time. The moves he had made towards the shore were actually failed attempts to get out of the river. Now he was cold and lacked energy to move. A group of people had to hold hands and make a line out into the river, to drag him out of the water.

This chapter explores how initiatives to seek, offer, and provide help is a central ingredient in coping with fallibility at work. First, it revisits two of the psychological phenomena discussed in earlier chapters—the bystander effect and the confirmation fallacy—to consider how they can contribute to an understanding why people are hesitant to seek and offer help. Second, it focuses on the perception of social cost as an explanation of why people might refrain from seeking help in critical situations at work. The starting point for that discussion is two examples from healthcare, one real and one fictitious, in which inexperienced professionals attempt to do things on their own, without help or support from colleagues. Third, it considers how systems of holding back can make people mute and passive in situations where they either need or are in a position to offer help. One person can withhold help to another, thinking that the other would probably not have gone out of his or her way to help if the roles had been reversed. When both have this assumption about the other, a system of holding back is in place, and it inhibits helping behavior.

Helping behavior among colleagues increase the likelihood that work units and organizations succeed (Grant, 2014; Grant & Patil, 2012; Kahn & Katz, 1966). Research on helping at work frames it as "prosocial, promotive and cooperative behaviors intended to benefit others" (Grant & Patil, 2012, p. 547). It includes assisting colleagues with work-related operations (Anderson & Williams, 1996), supporting colleagues who face personal problems (Kahn, 1998), and expressing compassion and care towards colleagues. Helping behaviors are fundamental building blocks of organizing, the process through which individual employees coordinate their efforts to achieve collective goals (Grant & Patil, 2012; Weick, 1979). They belong to the altruism dimension of what is called organizational citizen behavior, "individual behavior that is discretionary, not directly or explicitly recognized by the formal reward system, and in the aggregate promotes the efficient and effective functioning of the organization" (Organ, Podsakoff, & MacKenzie, 2006). The contribution of the current chapter is to tie helping behavior to the specific challenge of coping with fallibility at work.

1 Beyond the Crowd

The young man who could not get out of the waterfall by himself only got help when the crowd at the shore had diminished to only a handful of people. He had not been in constant need of help from the moment he stepped into the river. His capacity to handle the situation on his own gradually deteriorated with each effort to get out of the river by himself. Even if his condition got gradually worse, it seems likely that he to some degree was a victim of the bystander effect. When many people were present, none took any initiative to ask about his condition. As people started to go home from the bathing spot, diffusion of responsibility most likely decreased, as there were fewer and fewer people present who could share the responsibility of taking an initiative between them. Furthermore, the reasons for doubting one's own judgement that here was a human being in distress weakened when the number of other bystanders went down, and so the foundation for collective ignorance gradually diminished.

In previous chapters, the bystander effect has been used as an element in efforts to explain why people hesitate to intervene when they sense that a colleague is about to make or already has made a mistake. It can happen during an innovation process, where everybody can agree upon the importance of being able to fail fast, but still are mute about a growing concern that this might not be a good project plan or idea after all. It can also happen when safety is at stake, and many people know about a possible weakness in a procedure, of either a systemic or a personal kind. Research on the bystander effect makes it plausible that the higher number of people who know about the weakness, the less likely it is that anybody will take a step forward and identify it.

When it comes to bystander effects that inhibit helping behavior, it is really the home turf for knowledge about this phenomenon. As we have seen, it is well documented that the likelihood of receiving help in a critical situation tends to increase when the number of bystanders goes down (Darley & Latané, 1968; Fischer, et al., 2011; Darley & Latané, 1976). In organizational settings, there can be situations that are parallel to the one experienced by the young man stuck in the stream. Many can be witness to a colleague who is struggling at work, and each can interpret what they see in the light of the behavior of his or her fellow bystanders. With a high number of bystanders often comes an illusion of being only minimally responsible for taking an initiative to help, and a sense that the situation might not be as serious as initially thought, since everybody else is behaving as if everything is fine.

In the current context, it is noteworthy that the bystander effect apparently can be reversed by means of cues that raise public self-awareness in public settings. With the introduction of nametags and cameras, participants in bystander experiments have been more helpful when other people are present than when they are alone, indicating that they are guided by concerns about the impression they make on others (van Bommel, van Prooijen, Elffers, & van Lange, 2012, 2014). Reputation concerns and impression management lead to helping behavior. An unmonitored crowd offers anonymity and an opportunity to remain passive without fear of making a bad impression. In an organizational setting, this indicates that nametags and other ways of making bystanders identifiable can enhance the probability that somebody will take helping initiatives even when they are one of many. The presence of cameras is ethically problematic due to privacy issues, but the knowledge that the introduction of reputational concerns can reverse the bystander effect is nevertheless useful for efforts to raise help levels in response to fallibility at work. A person in need of help can also neutralize the bystander effect by pointing to one person in the crowd and ask him or her for assistance, instead of appealing in the general direction of all those present. That move can effectively puncture both diffusion of responsibility and collective ignorance, since it places one person in the spotlight and makes it clear that there is indeed a need for help.

Even the concept of confirmation fallacy can offer some explanation of both why a person in distress remains silent about his or her need for help, and why witnesses remain passive. Going back to the example from the river, the man stuck in the stream may have had an image of himself as a strong, muscular, mobile, and independent swimmer, who would never need help to get onto the shore after a dip in the river. The initial belief that he was capable to manage on his own may have remained with him, even after it was becoming obvious that it was false. Bystanders who took one look at him out in the river would also get a first impression of seeing an athletic person who appeared truly capable of taking care of himself. That assumption could survive the emergence of stark evidence to the contrary. In work settings, confirmation fallacy can also lead to initiatives to help colleagues who seem to need it, but in fact do not. The two alternatives to be conscious of, then, is that:

- A colleague who appears to be sufficiently competent and in control may actually be in trouble and need help.
- A colleague who appears to be in trouble and need help may actually be sufficiently competent and in control.

Research on confirmation fallacy suggests that we are slow to register changes in people's personal capabilities. Once we have supplied others with individual labels about what kind of people they are, we tend to be blind to obvious signs of negative or positive developments. It takes initiative to clarify whether first impressions are correct, and a colleague actually needs help, or not. That is what happened in the river episode, when a person on the shore finally took an initiative to inquire whether the man out in the strong current whether he needed help.

The most striking aspect of the incident in the river is the fact that the man in trouble did not ask for help himself, and had to be saved by another person's intervention. An appeal to a possible fixed self-image of being an independent and capable person cannot really function as the sole explanation. In the next section, attention turns to theories about how perceptions of social cost can inhibit people from seeking help. The act of asking others for help at work can be experienced as an admittance of defeat, of not being properly qualified for the job. Research on the real and apparent social costs of seeking help can clarify the extent to which a person is likely to be seen as less competent if he or she takes the step to ask for assistance at work.

2 Perceived Social Costs of Seeking Help

Reluctance to seek help in professional settings can create unacceptable risk and negative outcomes at work, since the solitary efforts of people who want to manage on their own can be inadequate in dealing with complex challenges. In the following, the point is illustrated through two narratives involving newcomers in healthcare who want to impress colleagues by demonstrating an ability to fix a problem without support from seniors. The first stems from an interview with doctor student Arne (not his real name), while the second is a fictitious account of what can happen when an inexperienced doctor attempts to be independent and autonomous in dealing with patient complications.

> I had a summer job at a mental hospital, and was eager to do a good job and impress the staff there. I thought it would give me exciting and relevant experience, a chance to get good references, and maybe weekend jobs for later in my studies. Looking back, I got a bit overexcited in some situations. I was very active and engaged in meetings with patients who were suffering from psychosis, and tried to talk and reason with them, when what they really needed was rest. My behavior was quite intuitive, and I could have asked colleagues for help, and whether I was doing the right thing. (Arne, 2016)

This doctor student shows the same hesitancy as the man in the waterfall to admit to himself that he cannot deal with the situation alone, and needs help. Both appear to have a need to demonstrate independence and individual strength.

> In one situation, I tried to convince a manic patient to reveal where she had hidden an ointment. Patients were not allowed to have medicine in

their room, and this patient refused to hand over this ointment. A doctor and a nurse were present, and I got a chance to show them my capabilities. What I realized later, was that if the patient would not immediately reveal the hiding place, she was too ill to be a patient at this unit. I should have calmly asked for the ointment, and if she refused, that would mean she should have a transfer to another hospital. The patient was quarrelsome, but not violent. I employed all of my skills of conviction, and we had a fierce exchange of words about the hiding place for the ointment. In the end, I won through and the patient handed over the medicine. I asked for feedback from the colleagues who had been present. The nurse claimed that I had been too active in the situation, and should have simply asked for the ointment, and left the room if the patient refused. The doctor said that I have handled the situation quite well. Later I heard that the nurse that gone to the unit leader and complained about my behavior, saying that I was not competent enough to be left alone with patients. I went into this job too eager to make a positive impression and should have been more ready to seek help from colleagues and become involved in the teamwork of the place. (Arne, 2016)

When an organization hires students and other inexperienced people, there is a need to clarify expectations and ground rules. What are the normal ways of interacting in this place? How do you balance collaboration and individual work? When is it acceptable to ask for assistance, and who are available to help? It is not uncommon for a young person to enter an organization with the mindset exemplified by the doctor student above, eager to impress colleagues and demonstrate competence, autonomy, and independence. If an organization wants to keep such solo initiatives at bay, it needs to communicate it in advance, and be clear about what is the normal and expected ways of working together.

In healthcare, transparency about the expected balance between individual and collective efforts is particularly important. Newcomers can have an understandable need to show colleagues that they are trustworthy and competent, but may end up causing harm in the process. We can imagine the following scenario: A young doctor is present one afternoon when a child patient arrives at the unit. This girl is scheduled for an operation the next day. When the doctor on duty is about to leave the unit for the evening, he asks the young doctor if there is anything he should know about before he goes home. The young doctor now has the opportunity to describe the condition of the child patient, but decides not to do so. He wants to cope with the situation on his own, without support from senior colleagues. During the night, a complication occurs with the patient, and the young doctor can again choose to consult a senior doctor, but decides not to do so, thinking that he can and should handle the situation by himself. The patient is sleeping, and the young doctor believes that the complication can be dealt with when she wakes up in the morning. The patient dies, and would most likely have survived if she had received proper, routine treatment during the night.

When a hospital faces a situation of this kind, it is a test of its ability to perform an autopsy without blame (Collins, 2001), or a calm and clearheaded analysis of the chain of events where the main attention is on causes, rather than blame. It appears that the young doctor has made passive mistakes in (i) not consulting the senior doctor before he went off duty, and (ii) not calling for help when the complication happened during the night. From one perspective, these are personal mistakes for which he is accountable, while from another perspective, they are systemic mistakes. A verdict depends on whether the hospital has clarified expectations about doing things together rather than one by one. Both the real and fictitious examples of junior doctors who want to impress have a past, present, and future dimension, with corresponding questions (Table 1).

It may be that the principle of seeking help when you are in doubt or at the limits of your own capabilities seems so obvious that it should

Table 1 Time frame for help seeking

Before	Critical quality moment	After
Did the organization properly clarify for the junior the normality and expectation of seeking help?	Should the junior be able to understand that he should seek help? Should senior personnel be more active in inquiring about the situation?	Will the student and the organization learn and improve practices of help seeking from the event? What are the consequences for individuals and the organization?

not be necessary to say it. However, patient safety in hospitals hinges on a deep, shared an understanding of this principle, and in meetings with inexperienced professionals, it seems reasonable to err on the side of over-communication rather than risk that they do not grasp the importance of seeking help when in doubt. Also, in the aftermath of critical event, it is possible to look at present routines and practices in order to consider improvements.

A person that refrains from seeking help from colleagues or others, even when he or she clearly needs it, is likely to perceive that the act of asking for assistance has some kind of social cost that they are unwilling to pay. Lee (1999, 2002) has proposed that there are three specific categories of social cost associates with seeking help. First, by asking for help one acknowledges incompetence and one's own inability to solve problems and find solutions by oneself. Second, a person seeking help acknowledges inferiority to other people in terms of knowledge, skills, and resources. Third, help seekers acknowledge their dependence on other people, and admit that they cannot complete a particular task along, but only through the efforts and contributions of others (Lee, 2002, p. 18). All of these categories of social cost have links to self-esteem. Admitting more or less publicly that you are not sufficiently competent, inferior, and dependent upon other people's contributions can disrupt a person's feeling of self-efficacy and being able to take care of him or herself. What will other people think of me, now that they have seem how dependent I am of help? These social costs can serve to explain the tendency to refrain from seeking help.

The doctor student's reluctance to seek help can be understood in the light of these theoretical propositions. He most likely wanted to avoid social costs in all three dimensions. First, he did not want to acknowledge incompetence, but instead had the ambition to make a good impression on colleagues and leaders at the mental hospital. Second, being a student he was already in some sense inferior to the other people in the workplace, and would not want to have the perceived gap in knowledge, skills, and resources widened even further by asking for help. Third, he acknowledges that he came into the organization with a plan to be perceived as an independent and autonomous person, someone who would deserve excellent references and offers of further assignments in the hospital. Asking for help would be detrimental to this plan. Only after feedback from the leader at the unit did he realize that the normal and expected behavior from newcomers was to seek assistance and be open about one's own shortcomings. Opportunities for further work at the hospital would have been greater if he had actively sought help from more experienced and competent colleagues.

In the fictitious case of the doctor who refrained from asking more experienced colleagues for help, we can imagine a similar set of reasons why he might have wanted to sort out complications with the patient on his own. He, too, is in a position where he wants to make a good impression and demonstrate that he can cope with complex cases on his own. All three dimensions of social cost are relevant to understand why someone in his position may avoid seeking help, even when the life of a child patient is at stake.

Gender differences can affect the threshold for seeking help. In a study conducted at a hospital, Lee (2002) followed the introduction of a new medication-ordering system, introduced in place of a system based on hand-written paper forms, and looked at how often people sought help from various sources when they encountered problems with the new system. She found that women were significantly more likely than men to seek help in such situations. That even held when comparing male and female doctors. Lee interprets these findings to mean that being competent, superior, and independent may be more important to male self-esteem than to female self-esteem. Gilligan (1982) proposed that women are socialized to value relational closeness and interdependence, while men to a stronger degree value independence and being able to look after oneself. There appears to be a gender difference when it comes to help seeking, and it can be important to acknowledge that, regardless of whether we consider that the causes are biological or social.

Another interesting finding in Lee's study is that tasks central to an organization's core competence, the ones that directly influence the organization's strategic advantage and competitiveness, are precisely the tasks for which the organizational members perceive the social cost of seeking help to be the highest. It appears to be harder and more socially costly, then, to seek help to perform tasks that people in the organization are supposed to be particularly good at. Lee (2002, p. 31) claims that acceptance of fallibility can be a key to improve the situation:

> This suggests that managers should pay particular attention to increasing help seeking in the organization's area of core competence, for example by decreasing social costs through increasing interdependence between employees, by encouraging employees to try risky experiments that may fail, or by establishing norms that making mistakes is acceptable.

At hospitals, one can thus attempt to decrease the social cost of seeking help, by encouraging a teamwork mentality. The doctor student interviewed about his summer job experience at a mental hospital indicated that he was slow to understand the team dimension, and only gradually understood that it was normal to seek help from other team members. In other organizations, the issue can be to find ways to introduce risky activities, much in the same manner as described in chapter three regarding Søbakken nursing home. What constitutes a reasonable tolerance for risk and harm will always depend on the local circumstances, but a common feature is likely to be that one finds a balance between active and passive mistakes, or between prescriptive and proscriptive dimensions of morality.

Another finding from research in this field is that the social cost of seeking help is lower than common perceptions take it to be (Brooks, Gino, & Schweitzer, 2015). The act of contacting another person to ask for help might even have a social gain rather than a cost. The study focused on the specific help seeking activity that consists in asking others for advice. Conventional wisdom and lay beliefs (as documented in two pilot studies for the main study) tend to be that asking for advice decreases perceptions of competence, but the results of the study indicate to the contrary that people tend to interpret acts of seeking advice as signs of high competence. The effect depends on the perceived complexity of the task: "When the task is difficult, asking for advice causes advice seekers to appear more competent than when they do when the task is not difficult; when the task is easy, asking for advice confers no benefit" (Brooks, et al., 2015, p. 547). It also makes a positive difference that the request for an advice is directed to the person who is going to assess the competence of the advice seeker. The dominant assumption appears to be that smart people ask for advice.

Perceptions of social cost can explain why people hesitate to seek help even in critical situations where their own capabilities are stretched. As we have seen in this section, emerging research provides us with reasons to reconsider establishes assumptions about the effect of help seeking on the perception of competence. Seeking help appears to have the potential to enhance social status, rather than diminish it. Knowledge in this field has the potential to change the way people think about fallibility and interdependence of work efforts, with a shift in focus from individualism towards teamwork and collective capabilities. It is likely to take conscious and systematic effort to establish a more team-oriented approach that acknowledges the limitations of what even the best-trained professionals can do on their own. Organizations can still expect that exceptionally gifted newcomers, with top results from top schools, will want to demonstrate their independence by managing on their own and not seeking help. Their leaders have an important task in communicating that it is perfectly normal and even required to ask for help and involve other team members in situations where they experience doubt and uncertainty.

3 Systems of Holding Back

When a person faces difficulties at work, help can be just around the corner, in the shape of a competent and experienced colleague who knows how to handle situations of this kind. All it takes is to get up from the chair and walk over to the colleague to ask for help. As we have seen in the previous sections, people tend to hesitate to do so in many contexts, and research on the psychological phenomena of the bystander effect and confirmation fallacy, as well as on the perceived social costs of seeking help provide input to understand and overcome the tendency to refrain from taking such initiatives. This section will consider another theoretical approach that also has the potential to explain the phenomena of not seeking or offering help. One thing is that the person who needs help at work remains at his or her desk instead of seeking help. Another is that the competent colleague may sense that a minor intervention can make a huge positive difference to the less experienced colleague, but still not make a move to offer or provide it. The ground cause for passivity in both cases may be what has been called systems of holding back (Hämäläinen & Saarinen, 2007).

A system of holding back is in place in a dyadic setting when person A and person B are both thinking along the lines of "I will not contribute to an improvement in this relation, because the other person is not willing to contribute". Both A and B would appreciate and benefit from an improvement, but each of them mistakenly assumes that the other person is not interested or would not make an effort. The result is that nothing happens. There is no movement in the direction of changing the relation for the better, since none of the people involved is willing to take the first step. The situation resembles that discussed in the previous chapter, the wait-and-see attitude (Dutton, 2003) that can prevent colleagues from speaking openly about failures and mistakes. The shared assumption there can be that "I will not be vulnerable and talk about my mistakes, because he/she is not going to be vulnerable and talk about his/her mistakes". In professional settings, there can actually be a mismatch in people's readiness to be open about failure, as doctor Bjørnbeth experienced with his first, failed attempt to establish a routine of talking about mistakes. He met genuine resistance to the initiative to establish a climate for sharing professional experiences of not getting things right (Bjørnbeth, 2017). In other setting, there can be systems of holding back, where the people involved actually have a common wish to overcome muteness about failure, but each mistakenly assumes that they are alone in wishing for it.

The researchers who have identified systems of holding back as a feature of human behavior believe that it takes systematic effort to overcome it. In a work environment where people are holding back, the negative spirals can grow stronger:

> The concept (of holding back) refers to mutually aggregating spirals which lead people to hold back contributions they could make because others hold back contributions they could make. We believe such systems are fundamental to human interaction – indeed, our conviction is that

human interaction has a tendency to slide into systems of holding back unless conscious effort is launched to counter this tendency. A negative dance of holding back will prevail unless it is countered time and again. (Hämäläinen & Saarinen, 2007, p. 26)

Efforts to disrupt systems of holding back can be Socratic in nature, and consist in raising questions about current practices. The Socratic motto "know yourself" can be interpreted as a reminder of the fact that we are relational beings. Knowing yourself is in this sense to become aware of the social systems you are a part of, and the extent to which you rely on contributions from others, and others rely on contributions from you. When you discern and contest systems of holding back, it can push individuals and groups in the direction of more constructive collaboration.

The philosopher David Hume has provided a vivid example of how two people can suffer from not overcoming initial reluctance to assist each other. One farmer notices that his neighbor needs help with his crop today, but refrains from helping because he does not expect the neighbor to assist him later when his crop is ripe:

> Your corn is ripe to-day; mine will be so to-morrow.'Tis profitable for us both, that I shou'd labour with you to-day, and that you shou'd aid me to-morrow. I have no kindness for you, and know you have as little for me. I will not, therefore, take any pains upon your account; and should I labour with you upon my own account, in expectation of a return, I know I shou'd be disappointed, and that I shou'd in vain depend upon your gratitude. Here then I leave you to labour alone: You treat me in the same manner. The seasons change; and both of us lose our harvests for want of mutual confidence and security. (Hume, 1975/1737, pp. 519–520)

One striking feature if this narrative is that each farmer appears to know about the other that there would be no return of services. Their assumptions about each other may actually be well justified and true, and so constitute knowledge. When there is a negative dance of holding back, there is at least movement, and the assumptions it is based on can be challenged. Hume's farmers appear to have stopped dancing, and ended up in a toxic deadlock.

In a system of holding back, the situation is initially one where farmer A thinks that "I will not offer to help him get the corn into the barn today, because he is not willing to help me tomorrow" and farmer B thinks that "I will not seek help from him to get the corn into the barn today, because he will not trust me to help him tomorrow". Assumptions about what other people are willing to do may be false. The more cemented relation that Hume describes may be what lies ahead if the system of holding back continues without opposition. Initially, false assumptions about a lack of willingness to help may gradually become true, as the relation deteriorates. We can distinguish between *fluid systems of holding back*, where it might not take much effort to expose false assumptions about the other's lack of readiness to help, and a *fixed system of holding back*, where it has actually become true that the two individuals are not willing to seek or provide help to each other. It is possible to imagine how Hume's farmers have been neighbors for a long time, and that there was potential for seeking, asking for, and providing help at the early stage. Thirty or so years later, the lack of initiative from any of them to cancel out the system of holding back has created a standstill where both are losers.

Time is also a feature in many instances of coping adequately with fallibility at work. If colleague A has spotted that B colleague has misunderstood a routine or adopted a bad habit, the longer A waits to tell B, the more awkward the situation is likely to become. We can imagine that B has misunderstood a particular written form they are using at work, and fills it in wrongly every time. A or other colleagues have adopted a habit of fixing the mistakes B makes, but nobody has taken an initiative to show him how the form is supposed to be filled in. If A picks a moment two years after these practices have been established to explain to B how it is really done, there are two things he or she will have to convey to B: (i) You have misunderstood the form, and filled it in wrongly, and (ii) I have known for 2 years without interfering and telling you. The thought of how awkward it will be to explain (ii) can contribute to more holding back from A and other colleagues in relation to B. The system of holding back can develop from being fluid to being fixed, unless somebody steps forward to turn things around.

The concept of holding back can serve to explain a range of instances where colleagues struggle to cope with fallibility. As illustrated with examples from aviation and healthcare, there can be critical situations where a mistake will lead to a negative outcome, unless somebody steps forward and intervenes to stop the chain of events that has been set in motion. People may hold back contributions they could make, based on assumptions about the extent to which the potential benefactor would have contributed if the roles had been reversed:

- I am not going to make him aware of his mistake, because he would not have made me aware of my mistake.
- I am not going to assist him in this critical phase of the project, because he would not have done the same for me.
- I am going to let him suffer through this on his own, because he would have let me suffer through a similar event on my own.

A common challenge in overcoming these systemic stalemates is to move from a passive mode to an active mode. As noted in chapter five, it is useful to distinguish between active and passive mistakes, between the mistake of doing something you actually should not have done, and the mistake of refraining from doing something you actually should have done. An active mistake is often salient by nature and tends to bring unwanted attention to the decision-maker, while a passive mistake can take place unnoticed, outside the spotlight. This asymmetry means that it is easier to get away with a passive mistake, compared to an active one. It can also strengthen systems of holding back, since passivity towards a habit of not supporting colleagues does not have the kind of obvious and tangible consequences that an active mistake can have.

The topic of this chapter has been how helping behavior can counter the challenges that occur due to human fallibility. In organizations where it is normal to seek, offer, and provide help to colleagues, the imperfect nature of professional capabilities is less likely to lead to bad outcomes than in organizations where people are more restrictive in those areas. The first example under scrutiny was one from a non-professional setting, where an athletic person stuck in a river stream refrained from asking for help. Similar situations can occur in organizations, when a person who apparently is competent and in charge of the situation, may actually need help, but be reluctant to ask for it. Three kinds of explanations of why people are reluctant to both seek and offer help have been discussed. First, bystander effects and confirmation fallacies can lead to passivity, in that both the person in trouble and the people watching may mistakenly think that this person is capable of managing on his or her own. Second, research on the perceived social cost of seeking help explains why the threshold for doing so can be high. It also exposes the perception to be dubious, in that studies show that help-seekers are often seen as more competent than those who try to do things independently and on their own. Third, systems of holding back can stand in the way of people seeking and offering help, in that people assume the other would not seek or offer help under reversed circumstances. There can be fluid systems of holding back, which can be challenged and exposed to be based on false assumptions about the other's willingness to make a positive difference, and fixed systems that have been allowed to develop over time and are harder to overcome. Conscious efforts to counter and challenge systems of holding back now appear to be central to any attempt to lay the foundation for adequate coping with fallibility at work.

References

Anderson, S. E., & Williams, L. J. (1996). Interpersonal, job, and individual factors related to helping processes at work. *Journal of Applied Psychology, 81*(3), 282–296.

Arne, S. (2016, 10th December). *Interview with student Arne/Interviewer: Ø. Kvalnes.*

Bjørnbeth, B. A. (2017, 18th January).*Interviewer: Ø. Kvalnes.*

Brooks, A. W., Gino, F., & Schweitzer, M. E. (2015). Smart people ask for (my) advice: Seeking advice boosts perceptions of competence. *Management Science, 61*(6), 1421–1435.

Collins, J. C. (2001). *Good to great: Why some companies make the leap… and others don't.* NewYork: Random House.

Darley, J. M., & Latané, B. (1968). Bystander intervention in emergencies: Diffusion of responsibility. *Journal of Personality and Social Psychology, 8*(4), 377–383.

Dutton, J. E. (2003). *Energize your workplace: How to create and sustain high-quality connections at work.* NewYork: Wiley.

Fischer, P., Greitemeyer, T., Kastenmüller, A., Krueger, J. I., Vogrincic, C., Frey, D., et al. (2011). The bystander-effect: A meta-analytic review on bystander intervention in dangerous and non-dangerous emergencies. *Psychological Bulletin, 137*(4), 517–537.

Gilligan, C. (1982). *In a different voice.* Boston, MA: Harvard University Press.

Grant, A. M. (2014). *Give and take: Why helping others drives our success.* London: Penguin Books.

Grant, A. M., & Patil, S. V. (2012). Challenging the norm of self-interest: Minority influence and transitions to helping norms in work units. *Academy of Management Review, 37*(4), 547–568.

Hume, D. (1975/1737). *A Treatise of Human Nature.* In L. A. Selby-Bigge & P. H. Nidditch (Eds.). Clarendon Press: Oxford.

Hämäläinen, R. P., & Saarinen, E. (2007). *Systems intelligent leadership systems intelligence in leadership and everyday life* (pp. 3–38). Systems Analysis Laboratory, Helsinki University of Technology.

Kahn, W. A. (1998). Relational systems at work. In B. M. Staw & L. L. Cummings (Eds.), *Research in organizational behavior.* Amsterdam: Elsevier Science.

Katz, D., & Kahn, R. L. (1966). *The social psychology of organizations B2—The social psychology of organizations.* New York: Wiley.

Latané, B., & Darley, J. M. (1976). *Help in a crisis: Bystander response to an emergency.* Morriston, NJ: General Learning Press.

Lee, F. (1999). Verbal strategies for seeking help in organizations. *Journal of Applied Social Psychology, 29*(7), 1472–1496.

Lee, F. (2002). The social costs of seeking help. *The Journal of Applied Behavioral Science, 38*(1), 17–35.

Organ, D. W., Podsakoff, P. M., & MacKenzie, S. B. (2006). *Organizational citizenship behavior: Its nature, antecedents, and consequences B2—Organizational citizenship behavior: Its nature, antecedents, and consequences.* Thousand Oaks, CA: Sage.

van Bommel, M., van Prooijen, J.-W., Elffers, H., & van Lange, P. A. (2014). Intervene to be seen: The power of a camera in attenuating the bystander effect. *Social Psychological and Personality Science, 5*(4), 459–466.

van Bommel, M., van Prooijen, J.-W., Elffers, H., & Van Lange, P. A. M. (2012). Be aware to care: Public self-awareness leads to a reversal of the bystander effect. *Journal of Experimental Social Psychology, 48*(4), 926–930.

Weick, K. E. (1979). *The social psychology of organizing*. Reading, MA: Addison-Wesley.

Open Access This chapter is licensed under the terms of the Creative Commons Attribution 4.0 International License (http://creativecommons.org/licenses/by/4.0/), which permits use, sharing, adaptation, distribution and reproduction in any medium or format, as long as you give appropriate credit to the original author(s) and the source, provide a link to the Creative Commons license and indicate if changes were made.

The images or other third party material in this chapter are included in the chapter's Creative Commons license, unless indicated otherwise in a credit line to the material. If material is not included in the chapter's Creative Commons license and your intended use is not permitted by statutory regulation or exceeds the permitted use, you will need to obtain permission directly from the copyright holder.

7

Ethics of Fallibility

Teacher A has a particular responsibility at her school for a group of pupils, aged fifteen, who are struggling either socially or with the school subjects, or both. One afternoon she has scheduled individual meetings with the parents of these pupils. In front of her now is the mother of Max, a pupil that has recently made considerable progress at school, both in the subjects where he has had difficulties, and in the social relations with other pupils. Max has become more integrated with the rest of his class and has stopped bullying other pupils. Teacher A expects him to continue on this positive path, and has great belief in him, based on his recent development in the classroom. When teacher A conveys the concrete steps forward that Max has made, and the expectations she has for him, the mother gets visibly proud of what she hears about her own son. She is probably not used to hearing positive things about his behavior. The meeting ends and the two women shake hands. Max's mother starts to walk down the corridor. It is at this moment teacher A realizes that she has made a serious mistake. The woman walking away from her is not Max's mother, but rather the mother of another pupil in her group, Alex. The papers about both pupils were on her desk when the mother turned up for the meeting, and she grabbed the wrong set of papers. In teacher A's mind, the person she greeted at the door was Max's mother, but now she has to admit to herself that it was not. Alex is a pupil steeped in trouble at school, a bully who is far behind the rest of the class in most subjects. The words teacher A has used to describe Max's progress in no way fits with the development Alex has had.

What should teacher A do now? She can either pursue the mother to acknowledge the mistake, or not. The previous chapter launched the principle of immediate acknowledgement: When you realize that your decision or behavior has caused harm, admit it and take responsibility immediately. The principle is not directly applicable in teacher A's situation. Her mistake has not yet caused harm, and may not do so later either. Immediate acknowledgment is nevertheless a viable option, and may be the right and proper thing to do. It depends in part on the foreseeable outcomes of telling and not telling. Alex's mother is on her way home, where she will probably tell her son that teacher A has high expectations for him. That may actually give him a positive and energizing experience, the opposite of harm. Even so, teacher A has to consider the ethical dimensions of the situation and to what extent she owes it to Alex and her mother, and to the school, to be open about the mistake she has made.

This chapter explores the normative and descriptive dimensions of an ethics of fallibility. The normative dimension is discussed from teacher A's mistaken identity case, in light of alternative justifications for acknowledging the mistake and not. The normative traditions of consequentialism and duty ethics provide conflicting advice about what teacher A and people in similar situations ought to do. Moral risk and the balance between prescriptive (do good) and proscriptive (avoid harm) considerations are at the heart of a normative ethics of fallibility, as noted in the chapter about events at Søbakken nursing home. This chapter outlines some theoretical resources available to formulate a normative platform for coping with fallibility, both with regard to what from a moral point of view should happen ahead of critical events where people are likely to make mistakes, in the midst of such events, and in their aftermath.

The descriptive dimension of an ethics of fallibility addresses alternative explanations to why people become involved in moral misbehavior, and often continue to be so once they have habituated a certain behavioral pattern. In an organizational context, it is particularly relevant to explore a phenomenon we can call moral fallibility, the instances where people act contrary to their moral convictions and values, first hesitantly and with some distress, later out of habit. One kind of explanation builds of virtue ethics, and sees moral wrongdoing at work as an indication of character defects and weakness of will, while another kind of explanation points to circumstantial influences on decision-making and behavior. Both belong under the heading of descriptive ethics, where the aim is to explain rather than to justify what people do. The main example under discussion will be from a turnaround process in Norsk Gjenvinning, a Norwegian waste management company, where work has been done to address instances of moral misbehavior. Material for the discussion will come from a Harvard Business School Case Study of the company (Serafeim & Gombos, 2015) and from an interview with the CEO Erik Osmundsen (2017).

The ethics of fallibility proposed here takes into account both normative and descriptive dimensions of human behavior. In the final section of the chapter, the two are combined in a stance on forgiveness. Considerations of whether a person who has made a moral mistake ought to be forgiven (a normative issue) can be informed by knowledge about why people make such mistakes (a descriptive issue).

1   The Good and the Right

Alex's mother is disappearing down the corridor and teacher A needs to decide whether to go after her to admit her mistake, or not. She can also postpone the decision about disclosure until tomorrow, or later.

If teacher A thinks solely in terms of self-interest in this situation, it is likely that she will keep the knowledge about the mistaken identity to herself. She is the only person in the world who knows about the mistake, and it is hard to see how anybody else will ever find out if she remains silent. The mistake will reflect badly on her professionalism, and she may come on the receiving end of repercussions or reprimands from her leader. Colleagues will most likely think badly of her. From a self-interest perspective, then, it appears that the best thing is to keep the knowledge about the mistake to herself.

From a perspective of professional ethics, teacher A should prioritize the pupil's interest over her own. As noted in the previous chapter, conflicts of interest are at the core of ethics in profession (Nanda, 2002). The professional more or less explicitly says to the client, patient, or pupil: "Trust me; although my self-interest may dictate other actions, I undertake to serve in your best interest." In teacher A's case, then, the professionally right thing to do in the aftermath of a mistake is to ask what would be in the pupil's best interest. Is it in Alex's best interest that he and his mother gets to know that the positive words about progress were actually about another pupil, and not about him? Is it in his best interest to get the truth, or to remain under the illusion that his teacher has seen progress in his development, and thinks he will continue to take social and subject related strides forward?

The discussion of moral risk in chapter three is also relevant with regard to the situation teacher A faces, and in the more general context of establishing a normative ethics of fallibility. Teacher A may wonder whether her leader and her colleagues will stand by her if she admits to the mistake, or whether she will be isolated and must defend herself alone. She has committed an active mistake, in doing something she should not have done. Keeping quiet about it might be viewed as a passive mistake, not being open about a mistake she should admit to the affected persons. There is also an element of balancing between a proscriptive (do no harm) and a prescriptive (do good) stance towards the pupil and his mother, but interpretations of facts and research indicating the probable effects of the alternatives can differ, and so also the perceptions of which of them are likely to be the more hurtful or beneficial.

The two main traditions in normative ethics are consequentialism and duty ethics. They offer different input to the situation teacher A faces, and what she should do. One way to describe the difference between them is to say that consequentialism gives priority to outcome (the good) over the quality of the conduct (the right), while duty ethics does the opposite, claiming that conduct (the right) is more important than the outcome (the good) (Kvalnes, 2015). Utilitarianism is the most common version of the former theory, and builds on the moral philosophies of John Stuart Mill (2002/1859/1863) and Jeremy Bentham (1970/1789). It claims that the decision-maker should always seek to maximize the overall sum of utility for all those affected by the choice at hand, and thus base the decision on a kind of cost-benefit analysis on behalf of all stakeholders. Duty ethics, based on Immanuel Kant's moral philosophy, holds that there are moral values that should never be sacrificed in the name of a good outcome. Human dignity, fairness, honesty, and respect, should always have priority over considerations about common utility, according to this line of thinking (Kant, 1998/1785).

Teacher A can seek advice from these two ethical traditions. Duty ethics will claim that she should choose the honest and truthful option and be open about the mistake towards Alex and his mother. Considerations about whether their lives will be better or worse depending on the disclosure or not are irrelevant from this theoretical perspective. In the here and now, we should be open with each other and not hide the truth, no matter what might happen next, because that is in line with core values of human dignity. Consequentialism, on the other hand, will claim that teacher A should consider the probable outcomes of her alternatives. Will it be harmful to Alex and his mother to continue their lives under the illusion that teacher A has seen great progress in his behavior at school, and is optimistic about his future, or will it be more harmful to them to have the truth about the mistake revealed? Answers to these kinds of questions will determine the consequentialist advice to teacher A.

At the moment in time when teacher A has to make her decision, there is no concrete way of knowing or predicting future outcomes for Alex and her mother. However, studies of the so-called Pygmalion effect indicate that teacher expectations about performances from pupils can become self-fulfilling. In one study, teachers at an elementary school were told that some pupils could be expected to be "intellectual bloomers" in a particular school year. Tests at the end of that year showed that the pupils identified in that manner actually had enhanced performances, compared to other pupils, even though they from the outset were singled out randomly. Positive expectations from the teachers, then, appeared to have a concrete, positive effect on how the students performed (Rosenthal & Jacobson, 1968). The effect has been documented in a later study (Boser, Wilhelm, & Hanna, 2014; Chadha & Narula, 2016), and also beyond the classroom. Pygmalion effects also occur in organizations, when leaders and colleagues express high expectations to their coworkers (Chandrashekar, 2016; Eden, 1990; Livingston, 2003).

With knowledge about the Pygmalion effect in mind, teacher A could choose to remain silent about the mistake, in the hope that Alex would respond positively to news about the high expectations from his teacher. Her mistake could then transform into a positive push for Alex. From a duty ethics perspective, this line of thinking misrepresents morality, in that it fails to give weight to non-negotiable moral values of honesty and truthfulness.

We can imagine a continuation of the story about teacher A, where she decides not to tell Alex's mother about the mistake. The mother goes home to her son, and tells him about the glowing positive appraisal from the teacher. In line with research on the Pygmalion effect, we can assume that what occurs next is a positive upturn in Alex's life at school. He starts to take schoolwork more seriously, and makes considerable progress both in the subjects where he has struggled previously and socially among the other pupils. Exposure to the teacher's positive regard and high expectations gives him a strong motivation to strengthen his efforts at school.

Such a positive outcome for Alex would not suffice to convince a duty ethics representative that teacher A was right in keeping the mistake to herself. From this theoretical perspective, moral luck (Nagel, 1979; Williams, 1981) can at most function as a label for the mistaken judgements people sometimes make, when they allow actual outcomes to overshadow the principled dimensions of a decision. According to duty ethics, we should always act in accordance with a maxim or rule of conduct that we can, to be universally applicable to these kinds of situations. Teacher A, then, should have asked herself whether she could will that every other person facing a similar situation applied the maxim of keeping quiet about the kind of mistake she has made. This Kantian line of thinking is similar to the one found in the Golden Rule, to treat others the way you want to be treated yourself. If teacher A had been the mother who had been mistaken for another, would she have wanted the teacher to reveal the mistake, or would she have accepted to be kept in the dark about it? Duty ethics in the Kantian tradition assumes that any consistent and rational person will end up prioritizing honesty over potentially positive outcomes in such situations.

In support of teacher A's decision, it can be noted that it was more than wishful thinking to assume that Alex could benefit from high expectations and praise, since research on the Pygmalion effect indicates that to be an expected outcome. She may even apply the Kantian maxim or the Golden Rule and conclude that she would accept similar treatment if she had been in the mother's position. During autumn 2016, the case was presented to special advisors in pedagogy, people who work closely with professionals like teacher A, They were asked to give an intuitive response to it. Around half the participants indicated that the right thing to do would be to explain the mistake to the mother, while the other half believed that teacher A should withhold that information. The case was used in three seminars with around one hundred professional participants each time, and there was an even split between a duty ethics answer and a consequentialist answer in all of them.

A normative ethics of fallibility can address a range of issues were people have made or are about to make mistakes. Questions of moral responsibility and right conduct can be raised at different moments in time about what one ought to do (Table 1).

The temporal structure can also illustrate the priorities within the two normative traditions. Consequentialism will seek information about likely outcomes in order to determine what the right thing to do is, and so is future oriented. Duty ethics, on the other hand, is primarily oriented towards the present, and on how moral values like human dignity, honesty, autonomy, and respect dictates what a person ought to do under the given circumstances, here and now. It can also to some extent be oriented towards the past, in taking into account what the decision-maker owe to the people affected by his or her conduct, based on previous promises and commitments. Even without a scholarly introduction to the two traditions, people tend to have strong intuitions about right and wrong, belonging to these theoretical categories. However, people

Table 1 Ethics of fallibility time frame

Before	Critical event	After
What are the morally right ways to prepare people (children, colleagues, professionals, etc.) for situations where they or others may make a mistake?	What are the morally right ways to intervene a course of events when a person is about to make or has made a mistake?	What are the morally right ways to cope with the aftermath of our own and other people's mistakes?

Woften do not remain consistent duty ethicists or consequentialists, but rather alternate between them when figuring out what the morally proper response to a situation would be. Only theorists in this area appear to be faithful to one particular ethical tradition over time. The rest of us tend to alternate, and be drawn towards outcomes one day and towards honesty and respect the next day, shopping around among ethical theories.

2 Moral Fallibility

"At some of our locations, we suspected hazardous waste was mixed with non-hazardous waste. We interviewed some employees about this practice, and they appeared not to see anything morally problematic with it, since competitors were also doing it, and it was a common thing to do. Our company also profited from it. Some said that they were only following orders from their bosses" (Osmundsen, 2017).

One aspect of an ethics of fallibility is what we ought to do in the face of possible and real failure and error, another aspect is what it is that makes us prone to commit moral mistakes. The quote above is from an interview with Erik Osmundsen, CEO of Norsk Gjenvinning (NG), Norway's largest waste management company whose owners and top management took the initiative to scrutinize and clean up the company's behavior with the aim to make it more sustainable. In that process, they came across examples of moral misbehavior among employees, and needed to find countermeasures to it (Serafeim & Gombos, 2015).

NG has around 25% of the Norwegian waste management industry's revenue. In 2012, the company handled about 1.8 million tons of waste, and had 40.000 customers. Since the introduction of new owners in 2011, the company has gone through a dramatic turnaround, where the aim has been both to become more cost-efficient, and to clean up activities and make them more sustainable. The new CEO Erik Osmundsen introduced a compliance program to systematize this effort. Nationally, NG has taken the industry lead in a development to see waste as a resource for recycling, rather than a problem to get rid of, and to make the industry itself more transparent. The company has activities all over the country, and had for a long time been structured in a way that made it difficult for upper management to evaluate local activities. Internal investigations exposed local practices of corruption. NG employees paid cash for hauls of mixed metal received at their waste drop-off sites, often not reporting the transactions properly. There were reports of thefts of metals from local industry sites, a practice that was incentivized by the industry wide practice of paying cash for metals at the sites (Serafeim & Gombos, 2015).

The most serious instance of morally questionable behavior detected in NG was the treatment and disposal of hazardous waste:

> At times, hazardous chemicals would be unwittingly mixed in with the non-hazardous waste supply. In other cases, NG employees would incorrectly code hazardous products for export. (Non-hazardous waste costs to ship were exceptionally lower than hazardous waste costs.) In the most egregious cases, some customers were unwilling to pay a higher price for the proper treatment of waste even after it was discovered that their waste included hazardous materials. Because their contract was already signed, the customers would refuse to pay the additional fees. This led some managers to ignore the issue and continue business as usual. (Serafeim & Gombos, 2015, p. 8)

One of the most difficult tasks for Osmundsen and upper management was to challenge and change the local practices regarding the treatment of hazardous waste. What they found during interviews with NG employees who had partaken in the practice was that they did not consider it to be morally problematic. On a personal level, it did not necessarily benefit them financially to let industry dump hazardous materials among the non-hazardous waste. It had become a habit to do so, and a standard justification was that everybody else was doing it. Changing the practice also appeared to make little sense to the employees, since the company was making a lot of money that way (Serafeim & Gombos, 2015, p. 9).

When studying this case from a vantage point outside the waste management industry, it is striking that the employees involved apparently did not see the questionable aspects of the practices. We can interpret this as another example of inattentional blindness, discussed in chapter two, illustrated with the gorilla experiment (Simons & Chabris, 1999). Even here, the individuals involved seem to be blind to important aspects of what they are doing, and blind to that blindness.

Moral fallibility is the name we can use for the phenomenon of acting contrary to one's moral convictions and beliefs. An individual may believe that adultery, tax avoidance, and nepotism somehow is morally wrong, but still engage in those activities, due to the weakness of will or some other explanation. Moral fallibility in organizations occurs when leaders or other employees make decisions and act in manners that appear to contradict what they generally take to be morally acceptable and right. A financial advisor may believe that he or she should put the clients' interest first, but still try to sell dubious products to them, to bolster personal bonuses. An athlete may consider doping to be morally wrong, but nevertheless take up an offer to use illegal substances to enhance performance. A waste management employee may be concerned about sustainability, and be a proponent of safe treatment of waste, but still let industry clients dump hazardous waste among the safe and recyclable waste.

If there are real cases that fit these descriptions, they illustrate that people can actually go against their moral convictions, and be morally fallible. However, one widespread assumption in the field of moral psychology is that when we come up against alternatives that conflict with our moral beliefs, we will dismiss them unless we manage to convince ourselves that those alternatives are morally acceptable, after all (Bandura, Barbaranelli, Caprara, & Pastorelli, 1996). The main idea is that "people do not ordinarily engage in reprehensible conduct until they have justified to themselves the rightness of their actions" (Bandura et al., 1996, p. 365). When facing an option to act against our moral convictions, then, we will either dismiss the option or revise those convictions to be able to proceed with the option, without conflict.

Rawls has described how individuals and groups seek "reflective equilibrium", a situation where there is coherence among our beliefs (Rawls, 1971). In that state of affairs, the beliefs we have about particular cases are consistent with our more general beliefs about right and wrong, and they provide mutual support to each other. Whenever there is a conflict with particular beliefs about what we ought to do and more principled beliefs, we tend to seek coherence by working back and forth to revise the beliefs, either the general ones or the ones about the particular case, until they are in equilibrium. Once we face an option do something that goes against our current principled beliefs, and are tempted or ordered to choose it, we can engage in a reflective activity to create coherence. Something has to give way, and that can either be the alternative of acting in that manner, or the general belief that it is wrong to do so.

Moral psychology offers conceptual tools to describe and analyze the tensions that can occur in such situations, and how we tend to deal with them. On one interpretation, what we have called moral fallibility never occurs, since we have the tendency to seek reflective equilibrium, and will revise either our particular or general moral beliefs, before we either dismiss the option or go ahead to act in a way that initially appeared to be wrong. According to this view, the financial advisor, the athlete, and the waste management employee mentioned above do not really act against their moral convictions or beliefs, since their actions indicate that they have managed to justify to themselves the rightness of those choices. They have been able to reshape their moral beliefs in manners that remove the initial conflicts.

Bandura et al., in the quote above, do acknowledge that people might act against their moral convictions, even though they do not "ordinarily" do so. It is reasonable to assume that some rest of the initial moral belief that it is wrong to prioritize self-interest over client interest, to use doping to enhance athletic performance, and to let clients dump hazardous waste in unsafe areas, remains, even after a process of convincing oneself that it is not. If so, the phenomenon of organizational moral fallibility is real and worthy of theoretical and practical attention. It can be important to understand the processes through which ordinary employees become involved in moral misbehavior, and act contrary to what they initially have taken to be morally acceptable and right.

Traditional virtue ethics would explain both inabilities to see morally problematic aspects of one's own practices, and the actual partaking in them, in terms of character defects and weaknesses. A person of firm and strong character would not become involved in such activities, and would not fail to see the immoral aspect of assisting industry in getting rid of hazardous waste in unsustainable ways. Recent empirical studies in social and moral psychology provide reasons to be skeptical of this character explanation, pointing instead to circumstance as a more reliable predictor of moral misbehavior (Ariely, 2012; Doris, 2002). Any person appears to be vulnerable to being blind to significant moral aspects of the practices he or she engages in. Once you come into a habit of doing things in a certain way, morally questionable aspects gradually become invisible. The idea that a person of firm character could never experience a development of this kind can create a false sense of strength and immunity among those who believe that they are in possession of stable dispositions always to do the right thing.

Theoretical contributions to moral psychology offer a vocabulary to give a more detailed account of the processes that can lead individuals and groups to adopt morally questionable practices. The next section will highlight how the concept of moral neutralization, developed by criminologists Sykes and Matza (1957) can be used to explain how decision-makers end up deviating from what they initially take to be morally acceptable behavior. This theoretical framework makes it possible to identify and categorize attempts to justify deviations from shared moral convictions and beliefs, and as such, it can be useful in organizational settings where the aim is to halt such developments and strengthen the barrier against moral misbehavior at work.

3 Moral Neutralization

The theory of neutralization challenges the dominant assumption that juvenile delinquents typically belong to a sub-culture whose members adhere to a set of moral values contradicting those held in regard by respectable, law-abiding citizens. Sykes and Matza (1957) described the young criminals as individuals who shared the moral convictions of the rest of society, but had been able to justify to themselves that they could not be blamed for those instances where they had broken the law. They introduced neutralization as the term for the justification processes that "precede deviant behavior and make deviant behavior possible" (Sykes and Matza, p. 666). Their theoretical framework has been adapted in different settings, to explain tax evasion (Thurman, John, & Riggs, 1984), normalization of corruption (Anand & Ashforth, 2003), insurance customer dishonesty (Brinkmann, 2005), software piracy (Bhal & Leekha, 2008; Siponen, Vance, & Willison, 2012), consumption of counterfeit luxury goods (Bian, Wang, Smith, & Yannopoulou, 2016), misconduct in marketing (Vitell & Grove, 1987), and unethical behavior intended to benefit one's own organization (Umphress, Bingham, & Mitchell, 2010). All of these studies focus to some extent on moral fallibility, and attempt to explain it as an outcome of a process of moral neutralization.

A person or group who engages in moral neutralization, first experiences some form of moral dissonance (Kelman & Baron, 1974; Kvalnes, 2015), a conflict between an option to act in a particular manner, and his/her/their moral convictions. In music, dissonance is the simultaneous emission of two or more sounds that are disharmonious. It is usually painful to the ear. The more general term of cognitive dissonance applies to the discomfort of holding conflicting cognitions. It was first used to describe the cognitive struggles of a UFO cult who believed in the impending apocalypse and faced a reality where that did not occur (Festinger, Riecken, & Schachter, 1956). The concept of moral dissonance describes a situation where somebody faces a situation where the person has the option to act against his or her moral convictions, and is tempted or ordered to do so. The situation can also be described as one where there is a lack of reflective equilibrium, and something has to give way to restore harmony among the person's beliefs.

A decision-maker has three main alternatives in overcoming moral dissonance. It is possible either (i) to dismiss the option and stay loyal to his or her existing moral beliefs, (ii) to revise and change the moral beliefs so that the described option no longer conflicts with them, or (iii) to reinterpret the situation to be different from the initial view that created the dissonance. The latter process can be categorized as moral neutralization.

Sykes and Matza identified five techniques of neutralization. The first is *denial of responsibility*, where the decision-maker sees himself as a victim of forces beyond his control, "helplessly propelled into new situations" and "more acted upon than acting" (Sykes and Matza, p. 667). The distinction between agent and pawn (Nygård, 2007), discussed in chapter one, is also relevant here. The decision-maker can deny responsibility by staging him—or herself as a pawn rather than as an agent. The second technique is *denial of injury*, where the decision-maker raises doubt about whether anybody will actually be hurt by his or her conduct. Delinquents may claim that the rich people they rob can afford it. Leaders can defend acts of lying as a reference person for an employee who is not functioning well in their own organization, claiming that the other organization is better equipped to motivate this person to do good work (Kvalnes, 2014). The third technique is that of *denial of victim*, where the argument can be that the part who might suffer due to this deviance from ordinary moral considerations, deserve it. It is a form of "rightful retaliation or punishment" (Sykes and Matza, p. 668). In a study of honesty in reference situations, leaders justified lying with claims to the effect that the other organization would have done the same to them, and probably already have, and so do not deserve moral protection against similar treatment (Kvalnes, 2014). Fourth, *condemnation of condemners* consists in pointing the finger at those who might criticize the act under consideration, and raising doubt about their motivation. From the perspective of the delinquent, "by attacking others, the wrongfulness of his own behavior is more easily repressed or lost to view" (Sykes and Matza, p. 668). Finally, the fifth technique of neutralization is *appeal to higher loyalties*, in which the decision-maker claims that other moral considerations or beliefs are more important than the one about to be sacrificed. In business, it can take the form of an appeal to the survival of the company. We had to cheat the customer a little bit, in order to save the workplace from bankruptcy.

The framework of moral neutralization has also been used to analyze the conduct of bankers and financial advisors ahead of the financial crisis in Iceland (Kvalnes & Nordal, 2017). Some of these decision-makers have gone to jail for misbehavior against their customers and the financial markets, taking risks that initially led to the collapse of all national banks, and to huge personal and collective financial losses. All five neutralization techniques appear to have been in use to justify the hazardous decisions, but also one kind of justification not captured by the original theoretical framework. The decision-makers frequently told themselves and others that none of their actions were in conflict with the code of conduct or regulations for financial activities. This sixth technique can be called *denial of rule violation*. The underlying assumption is that anything the codes and regulations are silent about is acceptable. The phenomenon can also be seen as a form of loophole ethics (Kvalnes, 2015), a strategy to identify and exploit loopholes in an ethical framework, claiming to be loyal to the letter of the code, and ignoring what may be called the underlying spirit of the code.

One analysis of the ethical roots of the financial crisis describes what can come after neutralization (Donaldson, 2012), where "bad practices can become institutionalized, and initial queasiness gives way to industry-wide acceptance" (p. 6). It thus identifies the period that may follow in the aftermath of a process where moral misgivings about a particular kind of behavior evaporates through neutralization. We can distinguish between three stages:

1. Moral dissonance
2. Moral neutralization
3. Normalization of morally questionable behavior

In organizations where the stakeholders are concerned about not getting to stage 3 in this process, it is possible to be aware of signs of moral dissonance, and to challenge neutralization attempts. It can be a part of the communication climate to bring attention to these phenomena, and to encourage people to speak up when they sense that colleagues or leaders are beginning to use neutralization techniques.

The idea that moral dissonance can give way to normalization of morally questionable behavior, through processes of moral neutralization, can be illustrated more or less anecdotally by pointing to concrete processes in organizations where that appears to be a reasonable explanation of known phenomena. It can also find support in neuroscience. One study has addresses how small acts of dishonesty can escalate into larger transgressions. Participants in an experiment that opened up for self-serving dishonesty became gradually more comfortable with lying. The researchers explain this in terms of brain adaptation. Initially, the lie registers as a dramatic deviation from the baseline, but with each new lie, the baseline changes, and the act of lying becomes normalized. The brain ceases to respond to the dishonest act as a shocking or unusual event (Garrett, Lazzaro, Ariely, & Sharot, 2016). In honesty research, the phenomenon has been called a "what-the-hell-effect" (Ariely, 2012; Mazar & Ariely, 2010), in an adoption of a concept originally used in research about eating, to describe people who succumb to temptations to violate a particular diet (Baumeister & Heatherton, 1996; Polivy & Herman, 1985). One violation opens up for further ones, as it changes the baseline for what you can do.

Even the moral fallibility of the NG employees who allowed industry clients to dump hazardous chemicals among the non-hazardous materials can be studied through the lens of moral neutralization. Viewed from a distance, this practice appears to be a clear example of serious moral misbehavior, in that it contributes to unrepairable environmental damage. When interviewed about it, the employees failed to see anything wrong with the practice, and argued that (i) everybody else in the industry was doing it, (ii) they were only following orders from bosses, and (iii) it gave the company a considerable profit (Osmundsen, 2017; Serafeim & Gombos, 2015). We can place arguments (i) under the heading of denial of responsibility, since the fact that it is common practice to do something appears to place it beyond decision-making and responsibility. Heath has suggested that the justification based on what everybody else is doing is not sufficiently captured in the original theory, and has introduced it as a separate, extra category of neutralization techniques (Heath, 2008). Argument (ii) is also to deny of responsibility, pushing it on to the bosses instead. Argument (iii) is an example of appeal to higher loyalties, placing the company's interest ahead of environmental interest. It is also an argument that places the activity in the category of organizational misbehavior that benefits the organization (Umphress et al., 2010; Vardi & Weitz, 2016), typically performed by employees who strongly identify with their organization, and are willing to break the law to protect its interests. Further studies of the actual justifications offered by NG employees is needed to document the extent to which moral neutralization has occurred in the processes leading up to habitual acceptance of unsustainable dumping of hazardous waste.

Studies in a range of disciplines show that our cognitive capacities are flexible, and that we can gradually come to accept and adopt behavior that initially appeared to be morally questionable. Organizational life can place us at the top of slippery slopes, where the first small steps into dishonesty and cheating can lead to major moral deviances later. One final example is from athletics. Tyler Hamilton was one of the cyclists in Lance Armstrong's team, and for a long period, he was in the midst of the lies and deceptions designed to make systematic doping to take place without detection. When asked about the cheating aspect of the team's activities, he responds:

> I've always said that you could have hooked us up to the best lie detectors on the planet and asked us if we were cheating, and we'd have passed. Not because we were delusional – we knew we were breaking the rules - but because we didn't think of it as cheating. It felt fair to break the rules, because we knew others were too. (Hamilton & Coyle, 2012, p. 95)

It is hard to say whether Hamilton and the others ever experienced significant moral dissonance before engaging in doping, but here at least any traces of moral misgiving about competing under the influence of performance-enhancing drugs have disappeared. Similar processes can take place in other organizations and work environments. It is likely that these are the main causes of moral misbehavior in organizations, rather than a weakness of individual character.

4   Forgiveness

During a visit to Iceland in the autumn of 2016, the author of this book asked a group of local citizens whether they would consider giving the bankers who had contributed to the financial crisis in 2008, and who had now served jail sentences for their involvement, the chance to start anew, with blank pages. Would they be willing to forgive these people, and let them put their past misbehavior behind them? The initial response from the group was that the thought had never occurred to them. It seemed so farfetched to imagine that those bankers could ever return in any kind of capacity of trust in the Icelandic society.

On the spot, the people around the table could provide a list of ten names of people who to their minds had severed ties with civic society forever. They were individuals who in their roles within the financial sector had pursued personal wealth at the expense of naïve customers and regulators. The gradual exposure of their dealings evoked responses of public rage. In this small society, everybody knows who the bankers are, and they have trouble walking the streets of the capital Reykjavik without experiencing negative interferences. Even though they have now served prison sentences, they have never admitted any mistakes. It is also a widespread assumption that they have hidden considerable assets abroad, giving them financial security for the rest of their lives. Forgiveness is therefore out of the question, according to the people I talked to. The start of any process of that kind would have to include a confession and a willingness to give up assets built up at the expense of ordinary Icelanders who had lost all their saving during the crisis. There was also a consensus in this group that the bankers had exposed their characters during their active years at the head of the financial sector, and revealed themselves as untrustworthy. To the bankers' defense, it can be noted that they were never invited to a reconciliation process, but faced criminal charges and were advised by lawyers to deny involvement in any of wrongdoing, in order to avoid or reduce prison time. The legally induced path of denial led them away from of a process that could have included at least partial acceptance of responsibility and blame.

Forgiveness has also been a topic in NG. At one point, the company issued an amnesty to the employees. If they came forward with information about misbehavior within a four-week period, they would not be penalized, even if they had been involved in these transactions themselves. CEO Osmundsen explained: "We had recently established a vision for the company, a set of values, and a code of conduct that every employee had to sign. The next step was to announce a period where people could come forward with information about misbehavior they knew about. Throughout December 2012, employees had the opportunity to tell us about previous and current practices that went against the code of conduct. If they were involved in it themselves, we would forgive them and let them continue in the company. If they decided not to inform us, and we detected wrongdoing after the amnesty period, there would be no mercy" (Osmundsen, 2017).

Top management in NG was soon tested on their ability to live by their words regarding the code of conduct and the promise of intolerance to code violations after the amnesty period. "We found out that one employee had allowed hazardous waste that should have been put in a landfill, isolated from the surrounding environment, to be used by a client at a construction site. This was a very serious breach of the code of conduct. He was a very competent person, and a good earner for the company, but we had to terminate his employment. This was a test of our resolve to walk the talk in connection with our recently defined values and code of conduct. The amnesty period gave everybody an equal and fair chance, and this person had not taken it. We had to show a commitment to the shared vision for the company" (Osmundsen, 2017).

The dismissal of an employee who has violated a newly introduced code of conduct does not hinge on the contested idea that character is the main explanation of misconduct. It can rather be seen as a move to strengthen the cultural foundation for responsible behavior. Approaches to moral fallibility in organizations can follow paths similar to those suggested for fallibility at work in general. We can assume that leaders and employees are prone to make small and large moral mistakes, more or less consciously taking shortcuts that go against their moral convictions. They depend upon a well-functioning barrier system in those situations, primarily in the shape of colleagues who intervene and bring their attention to the facts about what they are actually about to do. Even here, the communication climate affects whether the mistake leads to an unwanted outcome, or not. An effective barrier can break off the causal chain, and prevent the negative outcome from happening. Individuals who speak up and voice their concerns can influence the extent to which habits of overcharging clients, selling dubious products, allowing the industry to dump hazardous waste in unsafe environments, are formed or not. The more people who are witness to a slippery slope occurrence at work, the less likely it is that anybody will take action and protest against it, as we know from studies of the bystander effect. Even here, responsibility to take action is likely to be split into tiny parts, and other people's inaction is seen as evidence that there is nothing to be alarmed about. When the person who initiates misconduct at work is someone who usually behaves in morally exemplary ways, the colleagues witnessing it are likely to be slow or unable to pick it up, as suggested by studies of the confirmation fallacy. They expect more of the same from that colleague, and interpret his or her behavior in a favorable light, due to a more or less clean moral record up to now.

This chapter has outlined an ethics of fallibility consisting of a normative and a descriptive part. The former builds on duty ethics and consequentialist ethics as alternative approaches to how one should deal with situations where people make mistakes. Teacher A spoke glowingly to the wrong mother about her son, and later had to consider her next moves. She could listen to duty ethics, and do the honest thing of admitting the mistake, or take a lead from consequentialism, remaining silent in order to bring about the potentially energizing experience her mistake could create for the pupil in question. Further work is needed in order to provide a richer normative ethics of fallibility, and the two main traditions of ethics may provide conflicting advice even in other cases.

The descriptive part of an ethics of fallibility addresses why and how moral mistakes occur. We have seen that a person who experiences moral dissonance can engage in moral neutralization and attempt to justify to him or herself that the option in question is acceptable after all. The process can lead to a breakthrough, where moral misbehavior becomes the new norm. We are all vulnerable to becoming involved in processes of this kind, and depend upon colleagues, friends, family, and others to intervene to stop it from happening.

The normative and descriptive parts of this ethics come together in considerations about how organizations can counter and reduce moral misbehavior. The phenomenon of moral fallibility, or that people sometimes act against their moral beliefs and convictions, can be dealt with through the use of knowledge about its causes. Organizations can encourage their leaders and employees to have their eyes open for instances of moral neutralization, and to speak up when they notice them. A further challenge for researchers and practitioners is how to respond to people with a history of involvement in moral misbehavior. An initial response can be to claim that they have exposed their moral weaknesses once and for all, and cannot be trusted to change. Another is to look for realistic ways for people to reset their moral compasses, and re-experience moral dissonance in encounters with dubious alternatives, with the aim of giving people a new chance. The studies referenced in this chapter indicate that it is possible to incentivize people to refrain from organizational moral misbehavior, but they are unclear about the extent to which those who have transgressed can return to a state where they again experience moral dissonance at the thought of behaving in that manner. Icelandic bankers, Norwegian waste management employees, and others who have evoked moral criticism through their actions can be invited into a process where the aim is to forgive them. Such initiatives can gain momentum from an empirically informed descriptive ethics of fallibility that explains moral misbehavior in situational terms rather than by appeal to personal characteristics. We are morally fallible beings. Under unfortunate circumstances, anybody is capable of overstepping the boundaries for respectful engagement with others. This knowledge provides us with a platform for forgiveness, and for handing people a chance to be reinstated in our communities and start with a blank page.

References

Ariely, D. (2012). *The (honest) truth about dishonesty*. New York: Harper Collins.

Ashforth, B. E., & Anand, V. (2003). The normalization of corruption in organizations. *Research in Organizational Behavior, 25*, 1–52.

Bandura, A., Barbaranelli, C., Caprara, G. V., & Pastorelli, C. (1996). Mechanisms of moral disengagement in the exercise of moral agency. *Journal of Personality and Social Psychology, 71*(2), 364.

Baumeister, R. F., & Heatherton, T. F. (1996). Self-regulation failure: An overview. *Psychological Inquiry, 7*(1), 1–15.

Bentham, J. (1970/1789). *An introduction to the principles of morals and legislation*. Oxford: Clarendon Press.

Bhal, K. T., & Leekha, N. D. (2008). Exploring cognitive moral logics using grounded theory: The case of software piracy. *Journal of Business Ethics, 81*(3), 635–646.

Bian, X., Wang, K.-Y., Smith, A., & Yannopoulou, N. (2016). New insights into unethical counterfeit consumption. *Journal of Business Research, 69*(10), 4249–4258.

Boser, U., Wilhelm, M., & Hanna, R. (2014). The power of the Pygmalion Effect: Teachers'expectations strongly predict college completion. Retrieved from https://cdn.americanprogress.org/wp-content/uploads/2014/10/TeacherExpectations-brief10.8.pdf.

Brinkmann, J. (2005). Understanding insurance customer dishonesty: Outline of a situational approach. *Journal of Business Ethics, 61*(2), 183–197.

Chadha, N., & Narula, B. (2016). Pygmalion effect: Fostering performance among adolescents. *Educational Quest, 7*(1), 1–4.

Chandrashekar, K. R. (2016). The positive impact of Pygmalion Effect in the IT sector: An empirical study conducted in IT companies of Hyderabad. *Imperial Journal of Interdisciplinary Research, 2*(10), 936–941.

Donaldson, T. (2012). Three ethical roots of the economic crisis. *Journal of Business Ethics, 106*(1), 5–8.

Doris, J. M. (2002). *Lack of character: Personality and moral behavior*. NewYork: Cambridge University Press.

Eden, D. (1990). *Pygmalion in management: Productivity as a self-fulfilling prophecy*. Lexington Books/DC Heath and Com.

Festinger, L., Riecken, H., & Schachter, S. (1956). *When prophecy fails: A social and psychological study of a modern group that predicted the destination of the world*. Minneapolis, MN: University of Minnesota Press.

Garrett, N., Lazzaro, S. C., Ariely, D., & Sharot, T. (2016). The brain adapts to dishonesty. *Nature Neuroscience, 19*(12), 1727–1732.

Hamilton, T., & Coyle, D. (2012). *The secret race: Inside the hidden world of the Tour de France*. New York: Bantham Books.

Heath, J. (2008). Business ethics and moral motivation: A criminological perspective. *Journal of Business Ethics, 83*(4), 595–614.

Kant, I. (1998/1785). *Groundwork of the metaphysics of morals*. (M. Gregor, Ed.) New York: Cambridge University Press.

Kelman, H., & Baron, R. (1974). Moral and hedonic dissonance: A functional analysis of the relationship between discrepant action and attitude change. In S. Himmelfarb & A. H. Eagly (Eds.), *Readings in attitude change* (pp. 558–575). New York: Wiley.

Kvalnes, Ø. (2014). Leadership and moral neutralisation. *Leadership, 10*(4), 456–470.

Kvalnes, Ø. (2015). *Moral reasoning at work: Rethinking ethics in organizations.* London: Palgrave MacMillan.

Kvalnes, Ø., & Nordal, S. (2017). *Moral neutralization in the Icelandic financial crisis.* Work under review.

Livingston, J. S. (2003). Pygmalion in management. *Harvard Business Review, 81*(1), 97–106.

Mazar, N., & Ariely, D. (2010). Sequential influences on dishonest behavior. *Advances in Consumer Research, 37,* 143–145.

Mill, J. S. (2002 (1859/1863)). *Utilitarianism and on liberty.* Oxford: Blackwell.

Nagel, T. (1979). *Moral luck mortal questions.* Cambridge: Cambridge University Press.

Nanda, A. (2002). *The essence of professionalism: Managing conflict of interest*: Division of research, Harvard Business School.

Nygård, R. (2007). *Aktør eller brikke: Søkelys på menneskers selvforståelse.* Oslo: Cappelen Damm.

Osmundsen, E. (2017, 10th February). *Interviewer: Ø. Kvalnes.*

Polivy, J., & Herman, C. P. (1985). Dieting and binging. *American Psychologist, 40*(2), 193–201.

Rawls, J. (1971). *A theory of justice.* Boston: Harvard University Press.

Rosenthal, R., & Jacobson, L. (1968). *Pygmalion in the classroom: Teacher expectation and pupils' intellectual development.* New York: Holt, Rinehart and Winston.

Serafeim, G., & Gombos, S. (2015). Turnaround at Norsk Gjenvinning. *Harvard Business School Case,* 1.

Simons, D. J., & Chabris, C. F. (1999). Gorillas in our midst: Sustained inattentional blindness for dynamic events. *Perception, 28*(9), 1059–1074.

Siponen, M., Vance, A., & Willison, R. (2012). New insights into the problem of software piracy: The effects of neutralization, shame, and moral beliefs. *Information & Management, 49*(7/8), 334–341.

Sykes, G. M., & Matza, D. (1957). Techniques of neutralization: A theory of delinquency. *American Sociological Review, 22*(6), 664–670.

Thurman, Q. C., John, C. S., & Riggs, L. (1984). Neutralization and tax evasion: How effective would a moral appeal be in improving compliance to tax laws? *Law & Policy, 6*(3), 309–327.

Umphress, E. E., Bingham, J. B., & Mitchell, M. S. (2010). Unethical behavior in the name of the company: The moderating effect of organizational identification and positive reciprocity beliefs on unethical pro-organizational behavior. *Journal of Applied Psychology, 95*(4), 769.

Vardi, Y., & Weitz, E. (2016). *Misbehavior in organizations: A dynamic approach*. London: Routledge.

Vitell, S. J., & Grove, S. J. (1987). Marketing ethics and the techniques of neutralization. *Journal of Business Ethics, 6*(6), 433–438.

Williams, B. (1981). *Moral luck: Philosophical papers 1973-1980*. Cambridge: Cambridge University Press.

Open Access This chapter is licensed under the terms of the Creative Commons Attribution 4.0 International License (http://creativecommons.org/licenses/by/4.0/), which permits use, sharing, adaptation, distribution and reproduction in any medium or format, as long as you give appropriate credit to the original author(s) and the source, provide a link to the Creative Commons license and indicate if changes were made.

The images or other third party material in this chapter are included in the chapter's Creative Commons license, unless indicated otherwise in a credit line to the material. If material is not included in the chapter's Creative Commons license and your intended use is not permitted by statutory regulation or exceeds the permitted use, you will need to obtain permission directly from the copyright holder.

Conclusions

A choir stands on the podium, ready to perform Mozart's Requiem in front of an expecting audience. The conductor enters the hall and finds his place in front of the singers. He turns to the audience and acknowledges their applause. Then he gives his full attention to the choir, and provides them the tone from which they are supposed to start. Normally, the singers would adopt that tone immediately, and get ready for the task ahead. This time is different, because most of them immediately sense that the tone the conductor has given them is far too deep. Instant unease spreads among the members of the choir. If they follow the instruction and start the performance from that tone, this will end badly. The conductor himself does not note the hesitancy and confusion among the singers. He is unaware that he has made a mistake. What happens in the next second or two will determine whether the performance goes well or not. One or more of the singers need to step forward and intervene in order to stop the chain of events set in motion by the conductor's mistake. If none of them does so, they will soon be in the middle of a painful Mozart performance, unpleasant to their own ears and to those of the audience. There is no time to think the matter through, so either somebody makes an impulsive and discreet intervention, or they follow the conductor's directions into sour singing of Mozart.

This critical moment in a concert hall is a miniature example of how human fallibility can affect the quality of what people are trying to achieve together. Excellence in this performance depends on the detection of error, and an initiative to halt the course of events it sets in motion. Musicologist and conductor Mette Kaaby sees it as a nightmare situation, one that should not happen but may nevertheless be a reality. "A performance of Mozart's Requiem is all about collective precision. The choir and their conductor has put down hundreds of hours of practice together, to get the details exactly right. They are supposed to breathe, move, and sing together as one entity. The conductor needs to be sensitive to what happens among the choir members, and should be able to note signs among them that something is wrong. When that does not happen, it can create a musical crisis." (Kaaby, 2016).

The narrative about the conductor and the choir builds on an event that actually took place in a concert hall. What happened next was that one singer saved the day by discreetly correcting the tone from the conductor. The other singers started from that new tone instead, and the performance went well. There was a barrier system in place to stop the conductor's initial mistake from developing into a collective breakdown in the form of bad singing. The narrative also highlights other dimensions of coping with fallibility at work, as will emerge in the concluding reflections below.

This book has addressed how individuals, groups, and organizations can handle fallibility at work. It has highlighted how mistakes are not necessarily bad, since they can generate breakthroughs in innovative processes. Kaaby explains how there can be musical contexts where starting from a mishit tone can generate unexpected new dynamics among musicians. You open the wrong door, and explore what you find there, rather than turn around and insist on opening the door you were planning to open in the first place (Kaaby, 2016). Even in cases where mistakes lead to a bad outcome, there can be important learnings to draw from them, insights into how it is possible to do things differently and better the next time.

These closing remarks will identify three main categories of understanding to which the book contributes. Bringing together narratives and theory has provided insights regarding fallibility at work and (1) self-understanding, (2) process understanding, and (3) ethical understanding.

Self-Understanding

"Know yourself" is the Socratic motto introduced at the beginning of the book, and self-understanding emerges as a crucial component in preparing individuals for work setting where people make mistakes. It starts in childhood, where the scope of action boys and girls get to explore the world crucially affects their ability to cope with risk and adversity as adults. It matters how tight and wide the safety net is. If it is everywhere and protects the children from anything that might harm them, crucial learning opportunities are likely to be lost. Risky play is a key component in a stoical program to make children autonomous, resilient, and able to bounce back from failure.

The process of getting to know yourself can take an inward direction, where the aim is to figure out what really matters in your own life, but also an outward direction, where you take in the extent to which you depend upon other people to thrive and do well. The narratives in this book demonstrate how dependent we are on colleagues to take action and intervene in critical quality moments. They illustrate that we are relational beings, to a stronger degree than we perhaps are aware of and acknowledge. The choir narrative resembles those from aviation, healthcare, and industry about events that are likely to end badly unless there is an initiative from someone close to the decision-maker. Individuals who do take such steps tend to see themselves as agents rather than pawns, as beings with a responsibility and a scope of action to make a positive difference to the ways things turn out. They do not see themselves as spectators, but rather as participators in the processes that affect how things turn out. It also matters whether people consider themselves to have a growth mindset or one that is fixed and inflexible. Only the former approach a difficult situation, or even a failure, with the attitude that they can learn something from it.

Some of the narratives in this book are about ambitious individuals who want to demonstrate to themselves and their surroundings that they are independent and can manage difficult tasks on their own. The chapter on help discussed the reluctance some people—and men to a higher degree than women—have towards asking for support from others. We have seen that the actual social cost of asking for help tends to be lower than it is been perceived to be. The normal outcome may even be a social gain. You are likely to be considered more competent if you seek support in the process of performing a complex task, not less. These findings are important to convey to doctor students and others who enter working life with the assumption that they are supposed to tackle obstacles and deal with complexity on their own.

Process Understanding

A common feature in the self-understanding of professionals who partake in the narratives in this book is that they grasp the extent to which they depend on the activities of other people to do well at work. It is an attitude towards self and others that also give direction to process understanding, in that it emphasizes teamwork and collaboration rather than separate individual efforts. We can define it further by appeal to three components of a team oriented, collaborative process understanding. Dealing constructively with fallibility depends on:

A Barrier System

Reason's barrier model explains how mistakes can be detected and stopped from developing into accidents through the use of technological devices, rules and checklists, and human interventions. This book has highlighted the latter barrier element. People need to speak up when they sense that something is wrong, or somebody has made a mistake. The psychological phenomena of the sunk-cost fallacy, the bystander effect, and confirmation fallacy can make them hesitate, and thus pose a threat to the robustness of the barrier system. In the choir narrative above, there can be a bystander effect, in that many singers are present, and each of them may think that they only have a minor responsibility to intervene, and doubt their own judgement and assume that maybe it is only they who perceive the tone to be too deep. A confirmation trap can also be in place, if the conductor has a good reputation and no previous history of giving misleading instructions. The singers will then tend to expect the next instructions he gives to be correct, and neglect information to the contrary.

Countering Passivity

We have seen that a major process challenge in many work contexts is to counter passivity among those who are witnesses to mistakes. One obstacle is the well-documented phenomenon of omission bias, or of having a higher tolerance for bad outcomes of passive mistakes than for bad outcomes of active mistakes. A dominant assumption is that doing something that you should not have done is a more serious mistake than refraining from doing something that you should have done, even when the outcomes are more or less equally bad. When choir members experience that a conductor gives them the wrong tone, they can intervene at the risk of making an active mistake, or remain silent, at the risk of making a passive mistake. The most common approach in work settings appears to be the latter.

The chapter on Søbakken nursing home conveyed the need to balance risk and find a middle ground between moral hazard, where the decision-maker feels insulated against any negative consequences of his or her own actions, and moral paralysis, where the decision-maker feels that the entire burden of the negative consequences will fall on him or her. The latter phenomenon is under-discussed in research on risk-taking at work, even though it appears to affect work processes both in childcare and education, and in the treatment of elderly people. In both domains, moral paralysis can lead to passivity and unhealthy, professionally imposed restrictions on the scope of action for young and old people. Moral paralysis can occur in a range of other work settings, when employees choose passivity because they are afraid of making an active mistake, and thus end up making a passive mistake instead. One key contribution of this book—both in theoretical and practical terms—is to draw attention to the often unacknowledged and problematic tolerance for passive mistakes.

Other sources of passivity are the systems of holding back that make people into spectators in situations where they could have made a positive difference even by making a microscopic effort. In organizations, it makes sense to challenge systems of holding back, and be aware that they are tenacious. One colleague may assume about another that he or she would never be supportive in a critical situation, and the other may assume the same in return. The result is that none of them steps forward to help the other and both lose. It is possible to reveal those assumptions to be false, and move beyond them, but the systems of holding back are never overcome once and for all, but tend to reappear in new guises. This means that employees and leaders need to be alert to them, and take active steps to challenge the passivity they bring. In order to foster active engagement, we can appreciate, reward, and celebrate personal initiatives in critical quality moments.

Psychological Safety

The two doctors interviewed in chapter five both exemplify how openness about previous failures and mistakes can be a source of significant professional learning. When colleagues sit down together to analyze events that have not gone according to plan, with negative consequences, they build up a richer repertoire of possible responses to future events of the same kind. A precondition for honest conversations about one's own mistakes is psychological safety. The participants need to sense that what they have to say will not be used against them. There is a shared assumption that it is safe to be open about one's own experiences in not getting things right. The threefold definition of trust is also relevant as a component in this kind of safety. The person who shares the details of the mistake must believe that the recipients have the ability, benevolence, and integrity to use the information constructively. Narratives about mistakes make the narrator vulnerable, since it is likely that the information they contain can be used against him or her. Leaders have a particular responsibility for creating the psychological safety that makes the sharing of mistakes possible, by offering protection against repercussions. When done constructively, the emphasis is on the causes of why things went wrong and what can be done better next time, and not on attributions of blame.

Ethical Understanding

The narratives about fallibility at work also provide a source for ethical understanding. Events at Søbakken nursing home serve as an illustration of the extent to which the ethical emphasis in an organization should be on avoiding harm or on doing good. The leaders Borvik and Norlin shifted the attention from the former to the latter, thus prioritizing the residents' wishes for more activity and coming closer to life over protective measures. Creating awareness about the distinction between prescriptive and proscriptive ethics is in itself valuable, since it can generate rich discussions about priorities in the workplace.

One outtake from what doctor Westad told me is that it can make sense to immediately acknowledge a mistake, in order to stop victims from wrongfully blaming themselves for a terrible outcome. Both doctors who contributed to the discussion of learning from failure in healthcare see open talk about past mistakes as a genuinely future-oriented initiative, when it is motivated by a wish to learn and do better next time.

An ethics of fallibility can have a normative component, addressing how one should respond to mistakes at work, and a descriptive component, focusing on explanations of moral misconduct. Normative input can come from duty ethics and consequentialism, traditions that differ in their emphasis on whether moral qualities like respect, honesty, and fairness are more important than maximizing good outcomes. Descriptive input can come from studies in moral psychology that aims to explain why people engage in moral misbehavior. The two components can come together in a stance on forgiveness, or on the extent to which people who have morally misbehaved deserve to get a new chance. We have seen that this can be an ongoing and concrete issue, as in the turnaround at Norsk Gjenvinning and in the aftermath of the Icelandic financial crisis. One of the main findings in studies in moral psychology is that situational aspects have more predictive power than personal aspects, or that circumstances tend to influence behavior more than character. This tendency provides us with a general reason to forgive people for their misdeeds, since it raises doubt about the sharp distinction between good and bad people. It may be reasonable to expect some sort of confession or admitting to a moral mistake for forgiveness to take place. The parting idea in the final chapter of the book is that the process of forgiving (a normative endeavor) can be informed by insights from research in moral psychology (a descriptive endeavor).

Fallibility is a feature of human endeavors that we must learn to cope with, and the discussions in this book indicate that we can generate excellent outcomes together by realizing that we are relational, interdependent beings. Each individual depends upon others for support, encouragement, and help, but also for the constructive opposition in critical quality moments. When we overcome the systems of holding back, we are capable of producing what Esa Saarinen has called miracles of collaboration. Then we can shine and glow through the marvelous things we manage to do together, rather than one by one, as separate entities.

Future studies and reflections on fallibility at work will take place to the backdrop of automation, where more and more tasks are performed by intelligent robots that are capable of processing far more information than any human being, at a dramatically higher speed. These robots may not be infallible, but in many contexts, they are likely to perform far better than humans, since they do not get tired, exhausted, distracted, sleepy, angry, or exhilarated, states that can negatively affect the quality of our decision-making and behavior in critical situations. Automation opens up for safer traffic, more reliable medical diagnoses, higher precision in financial analyses. quicker proofreading, and so on. Robots are likely to outperform human beings in a range of contexts, thus making many of us superfluous in work settings. Our fallibility is part of the problem, but may also be a key to the solution, as we leave the activities that call for high precision and speed to the mechanical minds, and instead expand our scope of action in directions where trail and error are part of the thrill.

Reference

Kaaby, M. (2016, 20th May). *Fallibilty in choir settings*. Interviewer: Ø. Kvalnes.

Index

A
Active mistake 42, 43, 51, 55, 64, 67, 116, 124, 151, 152
Agent–pawn 3, 10, 14–17, 135, 149
Akerselva 101
Anti-phobic effects 2, 7, 8, 16
Anxiety 6–8
Ariely, Dan 133, 137
Attribution theory 15, 94, 95
Autonomy 5, 16, 41, 107, 127
Autopsy without blame 28, 108
Aviation 3, 23, 28, 60–63, 69, 72, 73, 75, 76, 86, 116, 149

B
Barrier model 60, 63, 68, 71, 150
Bentham, Jeremy 125
Bjørnbeth, Bjørn Atle 87, 91
Blame 16, 23, 26–28, 34, 42, 51, 64, 81, 82, 94, 108, 139, 153
Bolstad, Inga 21
Borvik, Kristine 39
Bottura, Massimo 26
bSafe 7, 8
Bystander effect 23, 29–34, 68, 89, 102–104, 112, 141, 151

C
Carlsen, Arne 40, 41
Carragher, Jamie 12
Childhood 1–4, 6–8, 11, 12, 14, 16, 17, 44, 51, 149
Cognitive dissonance 29, 30, 89, 134
Concorde fallacy 29
Confirmation fallacy 23, 29, 33, 34, 89, 91, 102, 105, 112, 141, 151
Consequentialism 122, 124, 125, 127, 141, 153
Courage 68, 76

Crew Resource Management 72
Critical quality moment 17, 73, 108

D

Danger 3–6, 9, 74
Denial of injury 135
Denial of responsibility 135, 137
Denial of victim 135
Descriptive ethics 123, 142
Design thinking 24
Diffusion of responsibility 31, 32, 68, 89, 103, 104
Dutton, Jane 81, 82, 84, 96, 113
Duty ethics 122, 124–127, 141, 153
Dweck, Carol 3, 10, 12, 13, 81, 93

E

Edmondson, Amy 22, 26, 28, 81, 95
Error 63–65, 68, 69, 71, 76, 86, 94, 129, 148, 155
Evolution 2, 4, 7
Excellence 148
Execution error 63, 64
External attribution 94

F

Feedback 14, 32, 33, 60, 61, 72, 75, 88, 107, 110
Fixed mindset 3, 12–14, 93
Forgiveness 123, 138, 139, 142, 154
Free-range kids 17

G

Gender 110
Gimmestad, Jarle 46, 60, 61, 91

Givers and takers 104
Gorilla experiment 35, 64, 131
Grant, Adam 102
Growth mindset 3, 10, 12–14, 17, 81, 93, 150

H

Halvorsen, Kristin 53
Harm 4, 6, 7, 9, 23, 40, 42–45, 47, 49, 51, 52, 55, 56, 64, 83, 86, 107, 111, 122, 124, 149, 153
Hazardous waste 129–133, 138, 140
Helping 54, 102–104, 114, 116
High-quality connections 81, 97
Hillsborough disaster 81
Hint and hope 69–72, 76, 89
Honesty 84, 85, 125–127, 129, 135, 137, 153
Hudson River landing 75
Hume, David 114

I

Iceland 11, 135, 138
Immediate acknowledgement 81, 83–85, 91, 92, 94, 96, 122
Inattentional blindness 33, 61, 62, 131
Innovation 22, 23, 25–27, 103
Integrity 55, 80, 83–86, 93, 153
Internal attribution 94

K

Kaaby, Mette 148
Kahneman, Daniel 29, 30, 33
Kant, Immanuel 125
Kohlberg, Lawrence 45, 46

L

Loss aversion 30

M

Mill, John Stuart 125
Moral development 45, 46
Moral dissonance 134, 136, 138, 141, 142
Moral hazard 40, 41, 49–52, 56, 151
Moral luck 40, 44, 47, 49–53, 55, 93, 126
Moral neutralization 133–138, 141, 142
Moral paralysis 40, 41, 49–52, 56, 151, 152

N

Norlin, Helén 41, 48
Normalization of questionable behavior 138
Normative ethics 122, 124, 127, 141
Norsk Gjenvinning 123, 129, 154
Nursing home 39–46, 52, 55, 56

O

Omission bias 43, 44, 55, 151
Organizational culture 69, 76
Osmundsen, Erik 123, 129

P

Parenting 5, 15, 16
Partnair accident 65
Passive mistake 42, 43, 51, 54, 55, 64, 67, 116, 124, 151, 152
Perception 33, 49, 61, 62, 93, 102, 112, 117

Pilot 16, 22, 46, 59–62, 65, 70–76, 88, 91, 111
Planning error 64
Pluralistic ignorance 31, 32, 89
Post-it 25, 34
Prescriptive ethics 44, 56
Proscriptive ethics 44, 56, 153
Protection 4, 5, 8, 12, 40, 50, 56, 135, 153
Pygmalion effect 125–127

R

Randjelovic, Mina 88
Reason, James 60, 63, 65
Reflective equilibrium 131, 132, 134
Rekdal, Kjetil 16
Relational attribution 94, 97
Resilience 2, 10–12, 17
Responsibility 12, 14–16, 21, 31, 32, 40, 51, 60, 67, 77, 82, 83, 85, 89, 92, 94, 95, 97, 103, 121, 122, 127, 135, 137, 139, 141, 149, 151, 153
Risk 2–4, 6–9, 11, 22, 40, 42, 44, 47, 49–52, 55, 56, 59, 68, 80, 86, 92, 96, 106, 109, 111, 122, 124, 149, 151
Rough-and-tumble 6

S

Safety 4, 5, 14, 17, 28, 44, 45, 47, 49, 60–63, 67, 69, 73, 74, 76, 81, 86, 95, 103, 109, 149, 152, 153
Salma 25
Sandseter, Ellen Beate 2–4, 6, 7
Saarinen, Esa 154

Scrapegoat 64
Senior-junior 88
Simons, Daniel 33, 62, 131
Skenazy, Lenore 5
Slips and lapses 63, 64
Social cost 86, 87, 102, 105, 109–112, 117, 150
Socrates 61
stoicism 10, 11
Sullenberger, Chesley B. 75
Sunk-cost fallacy 29, 30, 34, 89, 151
Surgeon 22, 73–75, 82, 87
Sustainability 131
Systems of holding back 102, 112–117, 152, 154
Søbakken nursing home 111, 122, 151, 153

T
Tenerife disaster 70, 72

Theiste, Morten 72
Trust 9, 46, 68, 80–85, 93, 96, 97, 115, 124, 139, 152

U
Upbringing 2, 9, 12, 14, 16, 17

V
Viagra 25, 34
Vulnerability 75, 91

W
Waste management 123, 129–132, 142
Westad, Stian 79

Open Access This book is licensed under the terms of the Creative Commons Attribution 4.0 International License (http://creativecommons.org/licenses/by/4.0/), which permits use, sharing, adaptation, distribution and reproduction in any medium or format, as long as you give appropriate credit to the original author(s) and the source, provide a link to the Creative Commons license and indicate if changes were made.

The images or other third party material in this book are included in the book's Creative Commons license, unless indicated otherwise in a credit line to the material. If material is not included in the book's Creative Commons license and your intended use is not permitted by statutory regulation or exceeds the permitted use, you will need to obtain permission directly from the copyright holder.

The manufacturer's authorised representative in the EU is Springer Nature Customer Service Centre GmbH, Europaplatz 3, 69115 Heidelberg, Germany. If you have any concerns regarding our products, please contact ProductSafety@springernature.com

Printed and bound by CPI Group (UK) Ltd, Croydon, CR0 4YY

23/03/2026

02076447-0016